ENDING WAR, BUILDING PEACE

Edited by
Lynda-ann Blanchard
and Leah Chan

SYDNEY UNIVERSITY PRESS

Published 2009 by SYDNEY UNIVERSITY PRESS
Fisher Library, University of Sydney
www.sup.usyd.edu.au

© Individual authors 2009
© Sydney University Press 2009

Reproduction and communication for other purposes
Except as permitted under the Act, no part of this edition may be reproduced, stored in a retrieval system, or communicated in any form or by any means without prior written permission. All requests for reproduction or communication should be made to Sydney University Press at the address below:

Sydney University Press
Fisher Library
University of Sydney, NSW Australia 2006
Email: info@sup.usyd.edu.au

National Library of Australia Cataloguing-in-Publication entry
Title: Ending war, building peace / editors, Lynda-Ann Blanchard, Leah Chan.
ISBN: 781920899431 (pbk.)
Notes: Includes index.
         Bibliography.
Subjects: Peace.
         Peace-building.
Other Authors/Contributors:
         Blanchard, Lynda-Ann.
         Chan, Leah.
Dewey Number:
         327.172

Cover image: Iraqi children at a makeshift refugee camp for internally displaced families in the Al Shuala district of Baghdad. © Donna Mulhearn 2004

Cover design by Pria Adam Mützelburg

CONTENTS

Foreword. Ending war, building peace v
Lynda-ann Blanchard and Leah Chan

Contributors ix

Introduction. Thinking war, crafting peace: a future for Iraq
and civil liberties in Australia xiii
Stuart Rees

Part One: The fascination with violence

1. The venerated and unexamined violence in everyday life ... 3
   Michael McKinley

2. Iraq, six years on: the human consequences of a dirty
   war 19
   Richard Hil

3. The human and environmental costs of the Iraq and
   other wars 33
   Sue Wareham

4. Spectacles of honour: barbarism within civilised reactions
   to public killings 51
   Sandra Phelps

5. The US invasion and occupation of Iraq and the
   implications for the Middle East: instability and the
   unravelling of US hegemony 65
   Noah Bassil

Part Two: Nonviolent alternatives

6. Between Iraq and a hard place 85
   Michael Otterman

7. Coalition of the unwilling: the phenomenology
   and political economy of US militarism 91
   Jake Lynch

8. Disarmament, demobilisation and rehabilitation:
   the pacifist dilemma 113
   Isezaki Kenji

9. The campaign against US military bases in Australia 121
   Hannah Middleton

10. The road to Fallujah 137
    Donna Mulhearn

11. The floating peace village: an experiment
    in nonviolence 151
    Yoshioka Tatsuya

Afterword. Learning and doing: the genesis of CPACS 163
Mary Lane

Index 183

FOREWORD

Ending war, building peace

Lynda-ann Blanchard and Leah Chan

The conference 'Iraq never again: ending war, building peace' held in Sydney, 15 and 16 April 2008, was made memorable by the motivation and passion of the participants. They were fed up with the belief that violence solves problems. They wanted to deliberate about peace in Iraq. In addition, the occasion was auspicious for other reasons. April 2008 marked the fifth anniversary of the beginning of the Iraq war. It was also the 20th anniversary of the founding of Sydney University's Centre for Peace and Conflict Studies (CPACS) and the 25th anniversary of the launching of the Japanese-inspired Peace Boat whose arrival at Circular Quay, Sydney Harbour coincided with the conference opening.

More than conference proceedings

This publication is born out of the conference. However, it is also born out of the theory and practice of CPACS in asking a central question: how does the peace studies perspective contribute to original thinking about the catastrophe of war? The introduction by CPACS founding director, Stuart Rees, sets up the dialectic of this edited collection: (i) how do we unmask our fascination with violence and, (ii) what might the nonviolent alternatives look like?

Therefore, part one of this book investigates the fascination with violence. In chapter one Mike McKinley begins from a position of "someone who believes it is possible to conceive of a just war – though almost impossible to find one historically". In confronting the truth about war McKinley explores themes such as commemorating violence and sacrifice; money in war; unrepresentative democracy; and divine justice. He suggests that we are so illiterate about nonviolence, we are only able to conceive of peace through war. The consequences of such a conceptualisation – including the human and environmental costs – are explored in the following two chapters by Richard Hil and Sue Wareham. The final two chapters in part one consider the dynamics of cultures of violence. In 'Spectacles of honour', Sandra Phelps considers 'barbarism' and 'civility' which, within cultures of violence, appear to be indistinguishable. In chapter five, Noah Bassil considers how the philosophy, language and practice of violence – exemplified in the US invasion of Iraq in 2003 – feeds 'radicalism', which according to the 2000 Sydney Peace Prize recipient Xanana Gusmao is a great obstacle to peace.

Part two of the book approaches nonviolent alternatives. In chapter six, freelance journalist and author Michael Otterman presents a pictorial representation of our 'humanness', a notion central to the philosophy, language and practice of nonviolence. Jake Lynch, in chapter seven, confronts the media as a pillar of power in our globally interdependent world and proposes ideas about peace journalism replacing war journalism. In order for that to happen, readers and writers of the media will seek to expose, and explore alternatives to, manifestations of cultural violence – such as the with-us-or-against-us statements of leaders – and structural violence, such as militarism and 'disaster capitalism'. Kenji Isezaki, in chapter eight, suggests an alternative narrative of international peace and security in terms of our responsibility to protect one another. In chapter nine Hannah Middleton introduces the academic/activist voice, and her narrative, a history of the Anti-American Bases Coalition Campaign, reveals a global "empire of [military] bases". In Middleton's analysis we unmask indirect or structural violence: 'what is not said' by governments, what is not reported in the media, what is not visible in active urban centres. As peace theorist Johan Galtung has remarked about the language of violence, "what is said is interesting, but what is not said is fascinating". The following two chapters are personal accounts of war and peace. Donna Mulhearn, in 'The road to Fallujah', takes us to the frontline of war as a peace activist, as a human shield. In chapter eleven, the Peace Boat story fills us with hope for a new story of humankind:

> Hope can neither be affirmed nor denied. Hope is like a path in the countryside: originally there was no path – yet, as people are walking all the time in the same spot, a way appears.[1]

Finally, Mary Lane's afterword tells such a story of hope as she recalls the prospect of "thinking slightly differently". She details the experiment and struggle of establishing academic peace and conflict studies in Australia's oldest tertiary institution twenty years ago.

Collaborative dialogue

This volume sets out to (a) avoid social scientific-style neutrality; (b) include a whole variety of perspectives – from academics of different persuasions, to poets, to activists, to refugee mothers; (c) address media constructions of war; and, (d) suggest what peaceful transformations look like. The collaborative approach to hosting the conference gives us the cue. That collaboration included the Sydney Peace Foundation, Macquarie University's Centre for Middle Eastern Studies and the Peace Boat's Global University. The participants, however, came from a much broader academic and community representation including Australian National University; Southern Cross University; Medical Association for the Prevention of War; University of Kurdistan Hawler; Tokyo University of Foreign Studies; La Trobe University; University of Western Sydney and so on. The collaboration included an orchestra of voices and instruments: from academics to activists, from politicians to refugees and to artists.

Ending war, building peace is about finding alternatives to violence. As the co-founder of the Conflict Resolution Network, Stella Cornelius, has remarked: "nonviolence is a beloved child who has many names". The director of the Sydney Peace Foundation, Stuart Rees, calls that child "peace with justice". He says, "to realise a vision of peace with

---

[1] From Lu Xun, to many the founder of modern Chinese literature, quoted in Kristof (1990).

justice requires inspiration and commitment" (Rees 2003, p. 82). That inspiration and commitment underpins the establishment and ongoing work of the Centre for Peace and Conflict Studies at the University of Sydney.

References

Kristof (1990). China's greatest dissident writer: dead but still dangerous. *New York Times*, 19 August, p. 15.

Rees, S. (2003). *Passion for peace: exercising power creatively*. Sydney: UNSW Press.

CONTRIBUTORS

Noah Bassil is the deputy director of the Centre for Middle East and North African Studies, Macquarie University and lectures in the area of international relations of the Middle East. His recent publications address issues related to the impact of colonial legacies on racial and ethnic identities in Darfur and the Sudanese state failure. Other research interests include Middle East inter-regional politics and the politics of representing the Middle East and Africa.

Lynda-ann Blanchard is a lecturer at the Centre for Peace and Conflict Studies, University of Sydney; executive member of the National Committee on Human Rights Education; executive member of the International Institute For Peace Through Tourism; and, consultant to the Conflict Resolution Network. She is co-editor of *Managing creatively: human agendas from changing times* (1996).

Leah Chan is a postgraduate student at the Centre for Peace and Conflict Studies and administrative assistant of the Sydney Peace Foundation at the University of Sydney. She spent five months as a volunteer in Guyana organising and facilitating health and education workshops and teaching literacy.

Richard Hil is a senior lecturer in the School of Arts and Social Sciences at Southern Cross University and an honorary associate of the Centre for Peace and Conflict Studies, University of Sydney. He has published widely in the areas of criminology, peace and conflict studies, juvenile justice and child and family welfare. Recent co-authored books include *International criminology* (Routledge 2007) and *Dead bodies don't count* (Zeus 2008).

Kenji Isezaki is professor of peace and conflict studies at the Tokyo University of Foreign Studies and lecturer at the United Nations University, Tokyo. He served as the Japanese Government Representative for Disarmament, Demobilization and Reintegration (DDR) in Afghanistan and as Chief of DDR in the UN Mission in Sierra Leone. He has published widely on UN peacekeeping operations and NGO management.

Mary Lane is a guest lecturer at the Centre for Peace and Conflict Studies and an honorary associate in the Faculty of Education and Social Work at the University of Sydney. Formerly a senior lecturer in social work, a major focus of her teaching and research has been community development, peace and conflict, and social work practice.

Jake Lynch is director of the Centre for Peace and Conflict Studies at the University of Sydney. He has spent the past decade developing and campaigning for peace journalism and practising it as an experienced international reporter in television and newspapers. He is convenor of the Peace Journalism Commission of the International Peace Research Association; a member of the executive committee of the Sydney Peace Foundation and of the International Advisory Council of the Toda Institute for Global Peace and Policy Research. He has authored numerous books, book chapters and refereed articles on peace and the media.

Michael McKinley is a senior lecturer in global politics at the Department of Political Science and International Relations at the Australian National University. His teaching, research and writing encompasses work on global politics, international terrorism, security issues in Australia's strategic environment, Australia's and United States' foreign policy, and philosophies of war and peace.

Hannah Middleton is a guest lecturer at the Centre for Peace and Conflict Studies and executive officer of the Sydney Peace Foundation at the University of Sydney. She is founding member and the national spokesperson of the Australian Anti-Bases Campaign Coalition. She is the Australian representative on the International Network Against Foreign Military Bases and on the Board of the Global Network Against Weapons in Space.

Donna Mulhearn is a postgraduate student at the Centre for Peace and Conflict Studies, University of Sydney. As a peace activist, she volunteered in Iraq as a human shield and later as a humanitarian aid worker. She has also spent four months in the West Bank of Palestine. A book about her experiences in Iraq, 'Ordinary courage: my journey to Baghdad as a human shield', will be published in February 2010.

Michael Otterman is a visiting scholar at the Centre for Peace and Conflict Studies. He is an award-winning freelance journalist and documentary filmmaker, and author of *American torture: from the Cold War to Abu Ghraib and beyond* (Melbourne University Press 2007).

Sandra Phelps is a visiting scholar at the Centre for Peace and Conflict Studies at the University of Sydney and head of sociology at the University of Kurdistan Hawler, Northern Iraq. Her current research interests include gender and ethnic intolerance within social groups and critical studies of peace, human rights and UN organisations to gendered violence.

Stuart Rees is former director and professor emeritus at the Centre for Peace and Conflict Studies and director of the Sydney Peace Foundation at the University of Sydney. He has worked in community development and social work in Britain, in Canada, in the War on Poverty programs in the USA and with Save the Children in India and Sri Lanka. He has published over one hundred articles and ten books including the poetry anthology, *Tell me the truth about war* (Ginninderra Press 2004). His other books include: *Passion for peace* (UNSW Press 2003); *Human rights, corporate responsibility* (Pluto Press 2000); *The human costs of managerialism* (Pluto Press 1995).

Tatsuya Yoshioka is co-founder and director of the Japan-based international organisation Peace Boat, which has been organising voyages for peace and sustainability education since 1983. He is a leading advocate within Japanese civil society and commentator in the Japanese media, as well as Regional Initiator of the Global Partnership for the Prevention of Armed Conflict (Northeast Asia).

Sue Wareham is president of the Medical Association for Prevention of War (Australia), which works for the elimination of nuclear weapons and for the promotion of peace and disarmament. She has spoken and written widely on these issues. In April 1999, she took part in an international delegation to Iraq to raise awareness of the devastating impact of economic sanctions on the Iraqi people and in December 2006 travelled to Lebanon with a delegation to document the effects of cluster bombs on civilian populations.

INTRODUCTION

Thinking war, crafting peace: a future for Iraq and civil liberties in Australia

Stuart Rees

As a conference introduction to 'Iraq never again: ending war, building peace', I explored two themes: (i) the age-old fascination with violence and war, and (ii) the crafting of a just peace for the people of Iraq. I also reflect now on the consequences for civil liberties in Australia when war becomes a foreign policy priority and if deliberations about a just peace do not occur.

The fascination with violence and with war

Those who were absorbed with aggressive, linear perspectives about the regime of Saddam Hussein were never serious about peace. On the contrary, their fascination with violence was a catalyst for war; and an appraisal of this destructive way of thinking would need to be made before any peace settlement for Iraq might be crafted (Rai 2002).

Linear or one-dimensional perspectives on ways to solve problems are characterised by a simplicity which is allegedly appealing because it is easy to understand. It involves 'either/or' views, are you 'good or bad', 'for me or against me'? It includes a tradition of hierarchical, top down decision-making which reinforces views – often racist – about the superiority of one group in relation to another.

In the early 20th century, the British treated Iraq elites as though they could not govern their country without British protection (Fisk 2005).

Oversimplified views persisted in the months preceding the March 2003 bombing of Baghdad. British and US government circles claimed that Iraq was a one man dictatorship which could easily be defeated and would welcome the imposition of democracy. Such a facile view held sway because intelligence services were poor and because leaders like Bush, Blair and Howard would not heed advice which did not correspond to their preconceived ideas. For example, before March 2003, Arabists from Cambridge University met with Prime Minister Blair. They reported that they had the impression "of someone with a very shallow mind, who is not interested in issues other than personalities of top people" (Steele 2008, pp. 25–27). In April 2004, fifty-two retired British diplomats, most of them career specialists in the Middle East, wrote an open letter to Blair deploring Britain's lack of prewar analysis. The diplomats said it was naïve to think that an invasion could create a democratic society. They said it was blind to assume that Saddam's removal would not boost the interests of Shi'a Islamists and strengthen the Islamist parties' loyalty to Iran (Cheehab 2006).

Simple reasoning about the merits of war was aided by deceit. Despite the conclusions of weapons inspection teams led by Hans Blix, the Bush administration insisted that Iraq had weapons of mass destruction (Blix 2006). In that administration's presentations to the UN Security Council, and in Prime Minister Blair's 'dodgy dossier' which said that Iraq had weapons that could reach Britain within forty-five minutes, lies followed lies. Deputy Defence Secretary Paul Wolfowitz said that he did not need direct evidence of the existence of weapons of mass destruction. Later he explained that this emphasis on weapons of mass destruction was merely the best bureaucratic reason for going to war. It was the reason which the American public would accept.

The US public's acceptance of the Bush administration's deceit may not have facilitated the drive towards war but it was never a hindrance. In the days following 9/11, that public was encouraged by a jingoistic media to believe that Iraq was connected to the destruction of 9/11 and was a threat to the security of the United States. A former Australian diplomat reported that of Rupert Murdoch's 174 newspapers, not one editorially opposed the war and once the invasion began, many of their commentaries became hysterically supportive (Broinowski 2007).

Another feature of one-dimensional linear thinking is evident in decisions to act alone, to go unilateral, to disregard international law. Under Prime Minister Blair's influence, the Bush administration sought UN cooperation when it seemed convenient but when the UN did not meet US wishes, it was derided. So emerged the US view that a legal framework was a hindrance to their policies, that unilateral action was the way to wage a war on terrorism. Within that war, Iraq could easily be included.

The refusal to learn the lesson that violence begets violence is another part of the pathology of war. Saddam Hussein was armed by the West and encouraged to wage war against Iran. Following the carnage of the first Iraq war – and no-one knows the extent of Iraqi casualties – the imposition of sanctions and no fly zones reduced Iraq to third world status. It became an easy target. The attack on Iraq in March 2003 occurred not because the country was strong but because it was weak. The cycle of violence gained momentum and perpetrators. It ranged from Saddam's tortures and mass executions to US arrangements for extraordinary rendition, from the numerous killings of innocents by suicide bombers to US security companies such as Blackwater murdering with impunity, from an Al Qaeda website showing the execution of an American captive to the abuse of Iraqi prisoners held by US soldiers in Abu Ghraib.

The other side of the violence begets violence pathology is a disinterest in the philosophy, language and practice of nonviolence. This disinterest amounts to an illiteracy which flourishes across countries and cultures. Through the centuries men have assumed that they can dominate women and abuse them in other ways. Similar top down ways of using power have been exercised by bullies in families, playgrounds, on factory floors and in boardrooms (Rees & Rodley 1995). Far more sinister ways of using power are exhibited by terrorists who maim and murder, and by armies which kill non-combatants and then, in Orwellian fashion, claim that they always act ethically.

At this point, it sounds as though some crude psychology will explain such destructive use of power in relationships. That is only half of the story. The other half concerns the eagerness of social institutions – education, the military, religion and politics – to adopt these abusive ways to promote policies and punish those who do not conform. Organised religion loves rules, seeks conformity and relishes punishment. The military breeds the belief that humiliation is one way to prepare soldiers and sailors for war. In his monumental work, *The prince,* Machiavelli sought to teach politicians that the possession of overwhelming force was the way to impress allies and enemies.

The merging of these institutional cultures with a mostly male-dominated psychology has forged the belief that force is a way to implement policies and that peace is some feminine notion which merits attention only when war has become too expensive. For these reasons, a first step in crafting a peace settlement for Iraq is to replace destructive ways of thinking with a multi-dimensional, life-enhancing perspective. Aggressive certainty will have to be replaced by questioning and reflection. Age-old assumptions about abuses of power will have to be replaced by a determination to be creative on behalf of and in association with others, hence my next few observations about poets.

A lesson from poetry: when will they ever learn

Assumptions about the value of violence can be so embedded in cultures that they are taken for granted but shifts to a different way of thinking can be helped by insights from poets. I'll begin with the Australian poet A.D. Hope's imagined plea, 'Inscription for a War' (Hope 2000, p. 129), from conscripts during the Vietnam War:

> Linger not, stranger; shed no tear;
> Go back to those who sent us here.
> We are the young they drafted out
> To wars their follys brought about.
> Go tell those old men, safe in bed,
> We took their orders and are dead.

In his poem, 'Men', the pacifist poet William Stafford reminds us of the consequences of purely militaristic ways of thinking (Stafford 1996, p. 40). Wars are followed by the erection of memorials for the dead, by collections for widows, and by claims that the surviving women and children have been made more secure by the latest fighting.

> After a war come the memorials – ...
>
> For a long time people rehearse
> just how it happened, and you have to learn
> how important all that armament was –
> and it really could happen again ...
>
> Then, if your side has won, they explain
> how the system works and if you just let it
> go on it will prevail everywhere.
> And they establish foundations and give
> some of the money back.

My protest, 'Against the latest war', depicts how an alliance of political, corporate and military mindsets encourages violence and makes it difficult to think creatively about peace:

> The inhumanity
> of the Iraq carnage
> is camouflaged
> by states spinning
> their versions of a truth
> that through the ages
> has served the needs
> of no-one except those
> who flaunt the trappings of office,
> sleep with corporate harlots
> and khaki mind sets
> in spite of poets warning
> 'It is not honourable to die for your country',
> or an author saying 'goodbye to all that'
> or even Noam Chomsky teaching
> how not to be fooled
> by those who want to control you.

Thinking and crafting peace

To replace this fascination with violence with an enthusiasm for the means of attaining a just peace requires a change in values and in thinking. It requires politicians, military personnel, journalists and the general public to shift from an interest in the military means of a notion like victory, to the hard slog of the day-to-day promotion of human rights. This shift depends on life enhancing ways of using power: respect for international law and a dropping of any go-it-alone, unilateral foreign policies. These are peace-oriented practices which could affect attitudes in all levels of government and civil society, in Iraq and neighbouring countries, in the United States and in all the other coalition parties to the Iraq War.

A plan for peace formulated with Iraqis would depend on a distinction between peace as an end to hostilities and peace with justice as in the attainment of citizens' human rights. The first objective could be achieved following a ceasefire but the daily necessities of clean water, a reliable supply of food and electricity, the experience of freedom of speech and of movement would take time to accompany an end to overt violence. The first objective could be attained within a short time frame. The second objective has much in common with community development goals with a minimum five-year span.

Proposals for peace would begin with an airing of several issues by Iraqis from all walks of life (Kucinich 2008; Transnational Foundation 2007). They must be at the centre of all dialogue about proposals for peace. I also assume that the future of Iraq cannot be considered in isolation from the politics of the Middle East. In this respect the United States cannot continue to operate a policy of double standards, one for Israel and one for other countries in the region. A peace with justice settlement for the Palestinians would greatly enhance the task of crafting a peace settlement in Iraq.

In addition to the premise that Iraqis will have to be at the centre of all dialogue, it should also be acknowledged that peace in Iraq is a collective responsibility and that an ambitious peace conference would need to be arranged by the UN, the Arab League, the EU and Iraq. That conference would set the goals for rebuilding a basic quality of life for Iraqi citizens: supply of water and food, resources for health and education, for administering the rule of law, and for caring for the elderly and disabled.

Peace settlement and humanitarian service

If human rights goals are valued, it follows that there can be no military solution to the catastrophe of Iraq. Human rights goals and other humanitarian initiatives would require the withdrawal of foreign troops, the dismantling of military bases and drastic reduction in the size of the US Embassy. The vacuum created by this withdrawal would be filled by a massive humanitarian service whose arrival would coincide with the departure of the military. Soldiers out, peace-building services in. A blueprint for such a humanitarian service already exists in the proposals for the creation of a permanent UN Emergency Peace Service (UNEPS) (Johansen 2006; Herro & Rees 2008; Herro 2008), which envisages a balance of men and women, of people from diverse ethnic groups and religions and with a range of skills. In the case of Iraq there would have to be a disproportionate representation of staff from Muslim countries. They would be nurses and doctors, social workers skilled in mediation, agronomists and engineers, plumbers and bricklayers. On the need to start re-building their country after the physical devastation, Iraqi citizens have said they will need not only Medecins Sans Frontieres but also 'bricklayers without borders' (Rees 2008).

An adjunct to the UNEPS-style proposal could include arrangements for a carefully planned exchange of postgraduate students from various professions and occupations who will have the skills to contribute to rebuilding Iraq. These internships would be for three, six, nine and twelve months. When Australian universities host overseas students, our experience is that such individuals complete projects with great industry, imagination and skill. Provided that the security of overseas contributors is guaranteed, the same student commitment could be applied in Iraq; and to provide an incentive for young Iraqis, they could also be given the chance to take up internships overseas.

Financial reparation for the destruction of war will have to be an early feature of the peace settlement. There is a precedent for the ways in which the amount of reparation can be estimated and paid. Following Saddam Hussein's 1994 invasion of Kuwait, various individuals, corporations and governments made claims for compensation and a commission of the UN Security Council estimated that $350 billion was owing. Now the payment for the destruction of war needs to go in the other direction, back to Iraq.

Another urgent form of reparation will be the clearing up of all the debris of war, the unexploded cluster bombs, land mines, the depleted uranium and the guns of all kinds. The collection and destruction of the means of waging war will be a highly significant step towards showing that security can be achieved by nonviolence and not by the age-old methods of killing and destruction. We are back to the appeal for a life enhancing way of thinking to replace the life destroying, one-dimensional, unilateral assumptions of so many violence-fascinated governments and their servants.

After the loss of as many as one million civilian Iraqi lives, the debilitating injuries to many more and the displacement of millions of refugees to Jordan and Syria and internally within Iraq, a process of healing will be as necessary as the mortar needed to re-build homes. To this end a peace settlement could include the creation of a Truth and Reconciliation Commission headed by respected Iraqis. The precedent of the South African experience shows, in Archbishop Tutu's words, that the means of reconciliation can be found in that middle way between general amnesia – forgetting all that has happened – and applying the Nuremberg principles of a victor's only version of justice (Tutu 1999). A Reconciliation Commission would not replace the country's restored systems of justice. It would evolve as a test of the participants' ability to be in dialogue and so rediscover that creative language and practice without which a just peace is impossible.

And civil liberties in Australia

These proposals for a peace settlement in Iraq are built around the precept that security will ultimately depend on social considerations not militaristic ones. But as a result of the war on terror and the associated war in Iraq, politicians felt encouraged to think that their country's borders and sovereignty would depend on limiting people's freedoms. They ignored the ideal that respect for sovereignty can also be built around policies to foster freedom and on the properties of nonviolence rather than the fear of more violence. These statements also have direct relevance to the state of civil liberties in Australia.

Since 2001, the Australian Federal Government has passed over forty pieces of legislation which erode citizens' civil liberties. This one-dimensional process began with the passage of the Australian Security Intelligence Organisation (Terrorism) Bill of March 2002. Those who drafted the legislation were playing the fear card and were obviously influenced by the even more fear-full US Patriot Act. The Australian legislation produced the new offence of terrorism, which could be punishable with up to twenty-six years imprisonment for an act made with the intention of advancing an ideological or political cause. ASIO agents were increased in number and given new powers to detain people for forty-eight hours, and to strip search anyone considered to have information pertaining to their investigation. They are not law enforcement officers and it is almost impossible to hold them accountable. Yet the Federal police do have law enforcement responsibilities and the size of their empire has increased remarkably under Commissioner Keelty. Their potential for ignoring civil liberties has increased in corresponding fashion. Their apparent withholding of information relevant to the charges against Dr Mohammed Haneef is a case in point (Ackland 2008 a,b).

There is a macho characteristic to those lazy ways of thinking which enjoy secrecy and which promote the notion that mine is bigger or better than yours. The 'mine' refers to legislation to deal with perceived threats of terrorism. For example, not to be outdone by the Federal legislation, the NSW Government passed its own *Freedom of Information (Terrorism and Criminal Intelligence) Act* which decreed that people could be protected by removing from the potential scrutiny of freedom of information any document which state agencies considered relevant to a terrorist threat. Not holding powerful people accountable is another feature of that top down one-dimensionality which is such an obstacle to debates about the meaning of peace and the means of achieving peace with justice.

Back to Iraq

The situation created in Iraq since the shock and awe bombing of March 2003 is widely acknowledged to be markedly worse than under Saddam Hussein's regime. This makes deliberations about peace an urgent priority. Those deliberations require a drastic shift in thinking in foreign and defence policy circles, in Australia and elsewhere.

The policy of militarisation – that possession of overwhelming power solves problems – flows from unimaginative, aggressive and lazy perspectives. Such destructive ways of thinking have occurred for far too long and at appalling financial and human costs, including an erosion of citizens' civil liberties. Visions of peace with justice are necessary to end the occupation of Iraq and to promise that country's citizens a far better future.

References

Ackland, R. (2008a). Another bundle of intrusions. *Sydney Morning Herald*, 4 January.

Ackland, R. (2008b). How the Haneef affair became a carry on coppers, *Sydney Morning Herald*, 22 August.

Blix, H. (2004). *Disarming Iraq*. London: Bloomsbury.

Broinowski, A. (2004). *Howard's war*. Melbourne: Scribe.

Chehab, Z. (2006). *Iraq ablaze: inside the insurgency*. London: I.B. Tauris.

Fisk, R. (2005). *The great war for civilization*. London: Fourth Estate.

Herro, A. (2008). It's time to give the UN some teeth. *New Matilda*, 24 November.

Herro, A. & Rees, S. (2008). Love Thy Neighbour. *New Matilda*, 29 May.

Hope, A.D. (2000). *Selected poetry and prose of A. D. Hope*. D. Brooks (Ed.). Sydney: Halstead Press.

Johansen, R. (Ed.) (2006). *A United Nations emergency peace service, New York*, Global Action to Prevent War (GAPW), Nuclear Age Foundation, World Federalist Movement.

Kucinich, D. (2007). *The Kucinich 12-point plan for Iraq*. Retrieved from kucinich.us/12-pt_Plan_Iraq.pdf.

Rai, M. (2002). *War plan Iraq*. London: Verso.

Rees, S. (2008). Bring on the bricklayers without borders. *New Matilda*, 25 April.

Rees, S. & Rodley, G. (Eds) (1995). *The human costs of managerialism*. Sydney: Pluto Press.

Stafford, W. (1996). *Even in quiet places*. Lewiston, Idaho: Confluence Press.

Steele, J. (2008). Ignorance, not ideals in Iraq. *The Guardian Weekly*, 2 January, pp. 25–27.

Transnational Foundation (2007). *Towards peace in and with Iraq*. Retrieved from www.transnational.org.

Tutu, D. (1999). *No future without forgiveness*. London: Random House.

PART ONE
The fascination with violence

1
The venerated and unexamined violence in everyday life
Michael McKinley

In the short analysis I am about to present, I speak within the Enlightenment tradition and its commitment to dialogue, debate and, above all, the scepticism and doubt which guides argument. Much of what follows will reproach not so much that tradition, but what that tradition has become.

In light of what I am about to say, I want to make two things clear: first, notwithstanding that I am speaking at a conference on peace and in a session justifiably and righteously critical of violence, I nevertheless assent to the proposition that, in some cases, self-defence, or the redress of gross injustice, requires violence. If I had to summarise my position, and I have to say that I am unhappy with the term myself, it is that of a 'just war pacifist' – someone who believes that it's possible to conceive of a just war – though almost impossible to find one historically. Second, and relatedly, nothing I say here should be taken as derogatory of the deaths and sufferings which Australians and others have incurred in many wars in response to the orders of governments that, in the national interest, they should fight, kill, destroy, and maybe die.

Specifically, then, what I will do is set out a series of observations and then suggest connections between them in a way which hopefully is empathetic to the objectives of this gathering. My argument is that what we tolerate, and even more, what we venerate, discloses who we are in general and what the true limits to our repudiation of violence are. Unless we examine these objects with a rigorous and undiscriminating scepticism, we cannot, even remotely, begin to understand our embeddedness in unacknowledged, but nevertheless approved, violence.

Commemorated violence

I start with an observation from Australia's national capital in Canberra. Along one of its more prominent thoroughfares – ANZAC Avenue – are numerous memorials to those who have served and died in the now many wars that Australia has participated in. The whole precinct speaks to commemorated violence. It is, of course, connected to the Australian War Memorial – an impressive building and one built with honourable intentions. I now approach it with a sense of deep foreboding as per the memorial's website.

At *KidsHQ*, children are challenged by way of a video, to "see if you can bust the dam" – as did the famous Dam Busters of 617 Squadron (AWM 2008b). Left unmentioned is the fact that the Dam Busters' raid was of dubious legality under the Laws of War as they existed, and was arguably a war crime. At the online shop, *Shop Spotlight*, you can order Bush Camouflage Bear with Disruptive Pattern Camouflage Uniform and/or a Vietnam Digger Bear (AWM 2008c). And in the memorial's *Discovery Zone* – the "hands-on [family-oriented] education space" made available through "cutting edge museum technology" – you can "experience the life of a chopper pilot in Vietnam" (AWM 2008a). The website shows a photograph of a 10-12-year old, in a junior flight suit, headphones on, strapped into the pilot's seat of a display Iroquois helicopter. But the choice is wide, both historically and in the sense of the virtual experiences on offer. An Australian War Memorial media release (2007) advises that, from July 2007, the "family-friendly interactive gallery experience will also include the ability to: "Dodge sniper fire in a First World War trench. Peer through the periscope of a Cold War submarine." The invitation, particularly to children, is to "climb, jump, crawl, touch and explore in all areas of the Discovery Zone … [which] … looks, feels and even smells different to the Memorial's other galleries." In Canberra, there is no peace memorial, or tribute to those who have pursued it, or even to those who have opposed war.

For those who might think that too much is being made of this well-funded popularisation of wartime experience and that overall it is at worst a neutral influence of the national culture, there I would refer them to reports in the metropolitan dailies that Australian Defence Force personnel in Afghanistan and Iraq were "ashamed of wearing their Australian uniform", because they were being assigned low-risk missions (Pearlman 2008). Regardless of the operational basis of the claim, it should be a matter of high concern that, in response to the report, the following comment was posted:

> Im 14 and an Australian girl and proud to be by the way!!! and i have always wanted to join the army from a very young age and to think that Australian's are signing up knowing they could die in frontlines for their country is a brave honerable thing to do. SO LET THEM!! [sic] (crewz, comment posted 27 May 2008).

Sacrifice

A second observation: just a few hundred metres from where we are meeting today (the Customs House on Circular Quay), there is another memorial, the ANZAC Memorial in Sydney's Hyde Park South. The central motif of the design is Rayner Hoff's *The Sacrifice*, officially described as a bronze group of sculptures depicting the recumbent figure of a young warrior who has made the supreme sacrifice; his naked body lies upon a shield which is supported by three womenfolk – his best loved mother, wife and sister and in the arms of one is a child, the future generations for whom the sacrifice has been made. According to the associated educational publicity, "it illustrates the sacrifice engendered by war, self-sacrifice for duty and the beautiful quality of womanhood which, in the war years, with quiet courage and noble resignation, bore its burdens, the loss of sons, husbands and lovers" (ANZAC Memorial, Sydney).

It is a striking sculpture – far more appropriate to its subject matter than the much larger project in Canberra – yet also disturbing because it deceives. It cannot speak of the event which took the lives that it commemorates – The Great War – and the politics of neurotic nationalism of a European order in decay, well described by Ezra Pound (1920) as "a botched civilization / an old bitch gone in the teeth."

It deceives, too, when it uses the term 'sacrifice'. As US Admiral Gene LaRocque had the honesty to put it, "I hate it when they say, 'He gave his life for his country.' Nobody gives their life for anything. We steal the lives of these kids. We take it away from them. They don't die for the honour and glory of their country. We kill them" (Turkel 1984, pp. 185–189). Many decades before, of course, Kipling (1919, p. 141), with ample reason, had written of the dead on the Western Front: "If any question why we died / Tell them, because our fathers lied."

Money in war

A third observation is that there is money in war. I don't wish to quote forever, but there are times and occasions when it is needed. Consider this – a soldier's recollection:

> War is just a racket. A racket is best described, I believe, as something that is not what it seems to the majority of people. Only a small inside group knows what it is about. It is conducted for the benefit of the very few at the expense of the masses.
>
> It may seem odd for me, a military man to adopt such a comparison. Truthfulness compels me to. I spent thirty-three years and four months in active military service as a member of this country's most agile military force, the Marine Corps. I served in all commissioned ranks from Second Lieutenant to Major-General. And during that period, I spent most of my time being a high class muscle-man for Big Business, for Wall Street and for the Bankers. In short, I was a racketeer, a gangster for capitalism.
>
> I suspected I was just part of a racket at the time. Now I am sure of it. Like all the members of the military profession, I never had a thought of my own until I left the service. My mental faculties remained in suspended animation while I obeyed the orders of higher-ups. This is typical with everyone in the military service.

> I helped make Mexico, especially Tampico, safe for American oil interests in 1914. I helped make Haiti and Cuba a decent place for the National City Bank boys to collect revenues in. I helped in the raping of half a dozen Central American republics for the benefits of Wall Street. The record of racketeering is long. I helped purify Nicaragua for the international banking house of Brown Brothers in 1909–1912 (where have I heard that name before?). I brought light to the Dominican Republic for American sugar interests in 1916. In China I helped to see to it that Standard Oil went its way unmolested.
>
> During those years, I had, as the boys in the back room would say, a swell racket. Looking back on it, I feel that I could have given Al Capone a few hints. The best he could do was to operate his racket in three districts. I operated on three continents (Butler 1933).

The writer was Smedley Darlington Butler, twice awarded the United States highest award for valour, The Medal of Honour. In contemporary times, nothing has changed.

Currently, members of the United States Congress have as much as $196 million collectively invested in companies doing business with the Defense Department and have earned millions since the start of the Iraq war, according to a new study by a non-partisan research group. The review of lawmakers' 2006 financial disclosure statements by Lindsay Renick Mayer (2008) at the Washington-based Center for Responsive Politics suggests that members' holdings could pose a conflict of interest as they decide the fate of Iraq war spending. To be noted is the fact that several members who earned the most from defence contractors have significant committee or leadership assignments, including Democratic Senator John Kerry, independent Senator Joseph Lieberman and House Republican Whip Roy Blunt. Overall, 151 members hold investments that earned them anywhere between $15.8 million and $62 million between 2004 and 2006.

According to Mayer (2008), "[s]o common are these companies, both as personal investments and as defence contractors, it would appear difficult [for an American investor] to build a diverse blue-chip stock portfolio without at least some of them." Even John Kerry, a Democrat who staunchly opposes the war in Iraq and a member of the Senate Foreign Relations Committee, is identified as earning the most – at least $2.6 million between 2004 and 2006 from investments worth up to $38.2 million. And the reaction to this in both the US media and here in Australia? It is best described as the Buster Keaton School of Political Analysis: genuine and total impassivity in the face of ethical, political, social, scientific and economic crises which threaten democratic government. "We the people", it seems, have become "we the governed".

Junk politics

Thus, a fourth observation: we live in the time of unrepresentative democracy, in which opposition parties are no more than the governing party in exile – to use a phrase increasingly common, this is a vacuous state we might now justly call the age of 'junk politics'. As one astute observer has written of another place – but a place towards which Australian social and political trends are increasingly vectored:

> Political parties are vestigial; the ideological temperature is kept as nearly as is bearable to 'room;' there is no parliamentary dialectic in congressional 'debates;' elections are a drawn-out catchpenny charade invariably won ... by the abstainers; the political idiom is a consensual form ('healing process,' 'bi-partisan,' 'dialogue') and the pundits are of a greyness and mediocrity better passed over than described. Periodic inquests are convened, usually by means of the stupid aggregate of the opinion poll, to express concern about apathy and depoliticization, but it's more consoling to assume that people's immense indifference is itself a wholesome symptom of disdain (Hitchens 1993, pp.12–23).

Child-like, those affected are deprived of a decent politically and historically informed understanding and remain forever in the thrall of what the French call *infantilisme*. Deprived, that is, of any understanding which would emphasise the continuity of things, they cannot comprehend the ways in which cherished values are subverted.

And today? By way of just one example, I have waited in vain for nearly seven years for someone to make the link between, on the one hand, current US behaviour, and on the other hand, the historical precedent set by the Spanish Inquisition. Despite that it holds torture to be legally proscribed and morally reprehensible, through the device of 'extraordinary rendition', the US has no difficulty with selected prisoners, clothed in orange overalls, being held without legal representation, accused anonymously in many cases, being interrogated, maltreated, and even tortured, and then deported illegally to another country which acts as an agent of the United States. Where, regardless of their guilt or innocence, they are without legal counsel, are tortured and frequently murdered in the process. Their deaths are excused by holding them to be an avoidable consequence of the need to combat a 'clear and present danger' to an imperial project requiring uniformity of belief and practice.

Is there not a remarkably unnerving equality between current US policy as outlined and the practices in Spain during the 15th and 16th centuries? Under Tomas de Torquemada, suspects were arrested without divulging the reasons for doing so and charged on the basis of testimony by anonymous witnesses or information which had not been communicated to the accused.

They were made aware that torture was a definite prospect and, if insufficiently forthcoming, actually tortured in their own account, and/or for the purpose of confessing knowledge of the crimes of others. Consider, too, that access to legal advice for defence was available but the advocates in question were no more than officials of the Inquisition, dependent upon, and working with it. Those convicted were forced to wear either a yellow or a black (depending on the sentence) penitential garment – the *sanbenito* – which signified infamy. Those wearing a black *sanbenito* (the condemned) were "relaxed" to the civil authorities – the Church being legally and morally proscribed from torture and execution – to be executed (Kamen 1998, pp. 189–210).

In writing this chapter, I have been unable to reconcile this refusal to confront what seems to be such an obvious historical comparison. At first blush it is exceedingly strange for a country whose dominant

Christian beliefs and traditions reflect the Reformation; then again, perhaps that is the explanation.

At issue here is an obscene, violent excess committed by states and their agencies which are directly responsible, indirectly responsible, or culpably inactive. Like all great institutional excesses, they first create their own powerful opposition, then the demise of the institution, and finally, its epitaph – along the lines borrowed selectively from Nizar Qabbani's banned poem of 1967, 'Footnotes to the book of the setback' (pp. 97–101):

> Friends,
> Our ancient word is dead.
> The ancient books are dead.
> Our speech with holes like worn-out shoes is dead.
> Dead is the mind that led to defeat ...
>
> Our shouting is louder than actions,
> Our swords are taller than us,
> This is our tragedy.
>
> In short we wear the cape of civilization
> But our souls live in the stone age ...
>
> Don't curse circumstances ...
>
> It's painful to listen to the news in the morning.
> It's painful to listen to the barking of dogs ...
>
> Our enemies did not cross our borders
> They crept through our weaknesses like ants ...
>
> We are a thick-skinned people
> With empty souls.
> We spend our days practising witchcraft,
> Playing chess and sleeping ...

> We praise like frogs,
> Swear like frogs,
> Turn midgets into heroes,
> And heroes into scum:
> We never stop and think.

In other words, we need to take the world as it is available to be known seriously – as deliberate and strategic, rather than an accidental and tactical construction. And if we do, the prospect is, in my view, clear and frightening.

Ur-fascism

My fifth observation is that the situation is worse than most of us think. Junk Politics is a stalking horse for something else, and the 'something else' is something we thought was over. In 1995, *The New York Review of Books* featured an essay by the Italian semiotician, Umberto Eco, titled 'Ur-fascism', by which he meant original, or eternal fascism – fascism not beholden to only the more familiar versions which we think have receded and are receding further.

In a reduced form, Ur-fascism is identified by the following common axioms:

> Parliamentary democracy is by definition rotten because it doesn't represent the voice of the people, which is that of the sublime leader.
>
> Doctrine outpoints reason, and science is always suspect.
>
> Critical thought is the province of degenerate intellectuals, who betray the culture and subvert traditional values.
>
> The national identity is provided by the nation's enemies.
>
> Perpetually at war, the state must govern with the instruments of fear.
>
> Citizens do not act; they play the supporting role of "the people" in the grand opera that is the state.[1]

---

[1] Lapham 2005a, p. 7. The point to abstracting Eco's defining characteristics of Ur-fascism through citing Lapham's essay is simply this writer's way of indicating that, when the (then) long-time and respected editor of Harper's Magazine is prepared

If we take a step backwards, in effect to translate ourselves to another level of abstraction, we understand that this ideology, or theodicy, was conceived in destruction and renewal, born of hope, in the spirit of surrender, and the imperative of a new beginning which Heidegger captured as the realisation that "[o]nly a god can save us", and Jung as "the right moment ... for a metamorphosis of the gods."

Divine justice

But my sixth observation is that Heidegger and Jung were wrong: God is not the answer, at least the God which informs so much of Western opposition to violence. Consider the Bible: in terms of an example of pathologically vengeful content, if the fundamentalist account of history found in the Old Testament is, as claimed, literally true, then equally it is deserving of Mark Twain's dismissal of it as "noble poetry ... some clever fables; and some blood-drenched history ... a wealth of obscenity; and upwards of a thousand lies". Where the same fundamentalists invoke the Almighty Father, Twain's rage is undiminished:

> The portrait is substantially that of a man – if one can imagine a man charged and overcharged with evil impulses far beyond the human limit; a personage whom no one, perhaps, would desire to associate with now that Nero and Caligula are dead. In the Old Testament His acts expose His vindictive, unjust, ungenerous, pitiless and vengeful nature constantly. He is always punishing – punishing trifling misdeeds with thousandfold severity; punishing innocent children for the misdeeds of their parents; punishing unoffending populations for the misdeeds of their rulers; even descending to wreak bloody vengeance upon harmless calves and lambs and sheep and bullocks as punishment for inconsequential trespasses committed by their proprietors. It is perhaps the most damnatory biography that exists in print anywhere (cited in Lapham 2005b, p. 7).

---

to risk the consequences of associating the Bush administration's "way of thinking and habit of mind" with fascism, despite the fact that this is done in the face of "the assortment of fantastic and often contradictory notions" that fascism embodies, then there are serious grounds for concern.

What Twain achieves through critical ridicule, others have reinforced philosophically by addressing the question of Divine Evil – by which they mean the evil which, if the relevant texts are taken seriously and literally, God himself commits.

In duration and intensity, these dwarf the kinds of suffering and sin to which the standard versions allude. For God has prescribed torment for insubordination. The punishment is to go on forever, and the agonies to be endured by the damned intensify, in unimaginable ways, the sufferings we undergo in our earthly lives. In both dimensions, time and intensity, the torment is infinitely worse than all the suffering and sin that will have occurred during the history of life in the universe. What God does is thus infinitely worse than what the worst of tyrants have done (Lewis & Kitcher 2007).

In the context of what I am saying, the significance of this conclusion is that it goes to the heart of the concerns of the matter – even to believers of a more relaxed dispensation in, say, the tradition of Erasmus.

To the extent that they, for now at least, practise a form of Christian humanism and tolerance, they can be thought of as unthreatening; but, at the same time, to the extent that they believe in and worship the perpetrator of divine evil, are they not themselves evil? Erasmus, after all, proposed only that theological disputes incapable of being settled during our earthly lifetimes should be left to the hereafter; this, of course, had to include the possibility of infinite punishment as I have just outlined.

And should this accusation apply whether the believers are those who, through their belief in their god, would also commit the same evil if commanded from above, or whether, in a spirit of humility, they consider themselves unworthy to execute such a warrant but give themselves to its author all the same? Under both dispensations they worship and thus endorse the author of eternal divine evil. It is seen as otherwise of course – as divine justice and the rightful damning of sinners; yet overall, is this not really a question of who does what, and under what rubric? If so, it remains the case that, for them, paradise is to be inhabited by 'committed misanthropes'.

The popularly understood New Testament offers little relief from outright rejection. Basically the problem is that the Christian Church(es) founded upon it are undifferentiated from many other human societies in that they subscribe to a belief in a "founding murder" – as well as in scapegoats "sacrificed to avert threats to the community". Thus, the ensuing community "builds itself around shared enmity and seals its bond by the sacrifice of the object of its fear" – an act of "creative destruction" which, in turn, brings forth a sacred, salvational outcome. The nature of the transaction is clear enough: something has to be destroyed in order that the people in question might live. The object, just as clearly, is to placate, flatter and bribe a violent god, or set of gods.

Life is thus oppressed by rites and sacrifices of "condoned violence" which are themselves products of hatred and "unreasoning contagions of panic". But these are nevertheless validated and controlled according to the illogic of the foundational act. Specifically, we might concern ourselves with the established belief that Jesus' agony, crucifixion and death are seen as the necessary sacrifice to buy off an aggressive Father, that Jesus is an "item of barter" in the exchange system, and thus, that God accepts sacrifices in "a logic of placation". In and of itself, this is an act of grand and deadly self-deception; when fused with the foundational myths of nation and state, the compound is sacred violence and the persistence of a violent political theology.[2]

In recent Western intellectual tradition, collegiality, civility, respect, tolerance, and perhaps affection have demanded and currently require a declaratory state of peaceful coexistence between all parties of all beliefs. This accommodation works very much the way quantum mechanics works in the discipline of physics; it isn't understood, but is used with great effect all the same.

The effect of the deep background is what worries me. It is at best a flawed accommodation but, I suspect, one that will not be challenged except by a few. And even then it will be met with the responses which

---

2 The use of Rene Girard's work in the above relies on the understandings provided by Gary Wills in his *Papal sin: structures of deceit* (New York: Image / Doubleday, 2000), pp. 303–07. The works of Girard he refers to are: *Violence and the sacred*, translated by Patrick Gregory (Baltimore: Johns Hopkins University Press, 1977), and *Things hidden since the foundation of the world*, translated by Stephen Bann (Stanford University Press, 1987).

Morris West (1996, p. 109) so insightfully captured in the Pontificate: examination will be deemed *non expedit* (it is not expedient), or *non e opportune* (it is not timely) or simply *fiat!* (surrender – let it be done thus!).

Final thoughts

We are fascinated with violence; equally we are illiterate in understanding how our own traditions and practices which ostensibly honour peace require a more suspecting glance than they are accorded. No discussion of nonviolence is possible without such a stringent examination of conscience. And it must be done in circumstances far from ideal, and which Bertolt Brecht foretold in his 1941 play *The resistible rise of Arturo Ui*:

> If we could learn to look instead of gawking,
> We'd see the horror in the heart of farce,
> If we would only act instead of talking,
> We would not always end up on our arse.
> This was the thing that nearly had us mastered;
> Don't yet rejoice in his defeat, you men!
> Although the world stood up and stopped the bastard,
> The bitch that bore him is in heat again.

References

ANZAC Day Commemoration Committee (1998). *ANZAC Memorial, Sydney*. Retrieved 14 July 2008 from www.anzacday.org.au/education/tff/memorials/nsw.html.

Australian War Memorial (2007). *Discovery zone to open soon*. Media release, 28 May, Australian War Memorial, Canberra. Retrieved 14 July 2008 from www.awm.gov.au/media/releases/download.asp?Media_Release_ID=99.

Australian War Memorial (2008a). *Discovery zone*. Retrieved 14 July 2008 from www.awm.gov.au/virtualtour/discovery.asp.

Australian War Memorial (2008b). *KidsHQ*. Retrieved 14 July 2008 from www.awm.gov.au/kidshq/technology/technology.asp?usr.

Australian War Memorial (2008c). *Shop spotlight*. Retrieved 14 July 2008 from cas.awm.gov.au/TST2/glbx.accept_login?screen_name=shop_pkg.pr_home&screen_parms=acid=&screen_type=BOTTOM.

Brecht, B. (1972). *The resistible rise of Arturo Ui*, adapted by G. Tabori. New York: S. French, p. 128.

Butler, S.D. (1933). Excerpt from a speech, as cited in The Wisdom Fund 2001, *War is a racket*, 11 September. Retrieved 14 July 2008 from www.twf.org/News/Y2001/0911-Racket.html.

crewz (2008). 'LET THEM!!', *Army chief reassures infantry troops*. Comment posted 27 May. Retrieved 30 May 2008 from news.ninemsn.com.au/article.aspx?id=569651.

Eco, U. (1995). Ur-fascism. *The New York Review of Books*, 22 June, pp. 12–15.

Hitchens, C. (1993). On the imagination of conspiracy. In *For the sake of argument*. London: Verso, pp. 12–23.

Kamen, H. (1998). *The Spanish Inquisition: a historical revision*. London: Folio Society, pp. 189–210.

Kipling, R. (1919). *The years between*. London: Methuen & Co., pp. 135–147.

Lapham, L. (2005a). Notebook: on message. *Harper's Magazine*, October, pp. 7–9.

Lapham, L. (2005b). Notebook: the wrath of the lamb. *Harper's Magazine*, May, p. 7–9.

Lewis, D. & Kitcher, P. (2007). And lead us not. *Harper's Magazine*, December, pp. 28–30.

Mayer, L.R. (2008). *Strategic assets*. Center for Responsive Politics. Retrieved 14 July 2008 from www.opensecrets.org/capital_eye/inside.php?ID=342.

Qabbani, N. (1986). Footnotes to the Book of the Setback. In Abdallah Al-Udhari, (Ed and Trans). *Modern poetry of the Arab world*. Harmondsworth: Penguin, pp. 96–98.

Pearlman, J. (2008). Ashamed to wear uniform. *The Sydney Morning Herald*, 27 May. Retrieved 29 May 2008 from www.smh.com.au/articles/2008/05/26/1211653939158.html.

Pound, E. (1920). *Hugh Selwyn Mauberly*. London: The Ovid Press.

Terkel, S. (1984). *The good war: an oral history of World War Two*. New York: Random House, pp. 185–89. As cited in W. Frazier, *The business of war*. Retrieved 14 July 2008 from ahealedplanet.net/war.htm#_ednref268.

West, M. (1996). *A view from the ridge: the testimony of a pilgrim*. Sydney: HarperCollins.

2

Iraq, six years on: the human consequences of a dirty war

Richard Hil

The Iraq war began on 20 March 2003 and 'ended' (according to President George Bush) on 1 May of the same year, only to be followed by an unfolding story of death and destruction unprecedented even in the Middle East. The invasion, code-named Operation Iraqi Freedom, was mounted by a self-styled 'coalition of the willing' led by the United States under the paper-thin pretexts of bringing freedom and democracy to Iraq and eradicating weapons of mass destruction (Bamford 2004; Rampton & Stauber 2003). We now know that these pretexts were false and that the invasion was inspired by a grandiose imperialistic vision of world domination as articulated in the infamous neo-conservative blueprint, 'The Project for a New American Century' (Kristol, n.d.). The invasion of Iraq was discussed by President Bush and his colleagues at a specially convened meeting on the evening of 11 September 2001. The attacks on the World Trade Centre in Manhattan had given the new administration all the justification it needed to mount what turned out to be an ill-fated war against a country that posed no immediate threat to the United States or its allies. International legal scholars were united in their opposition to the war, asserting that the invasion breached international law and failed to meet even the most basic requirements of a 'just war' (Sands 2005; Willis 2004; Frame 2004). Additionally, the war went ahead despite the mass protests of millions of people around the world, culminating in a march on 15 April 2003 when tens of millions of people protested against the impending war (Hil 2008).

Much has happened in Iraq since 2003. The initial phases of occupation were relatively calm as the coalition leaders basked in what looked like a rapid 'shock and awe' victory over a brutal enemy. But what became apparent very quickly – despite the attempt by the newly appointed "viceroy" of Baghdad, Paul L. Brenner, to claim a "new Iraq" (that was "open for business") – was that military and political leaders in the US and elsewhere had no post-invasion plan (Fisk 2003; Cockburn 2006). To make matters worse, Brenner – in the face of desperate pleas by his own advisers – embarked on a disastrous policy of 'de-Baathification' that resulted in thousands of former Saddam loyalists being thrown out of work (Chandrasekaran 2008). Such policies gave rise to deep resentment and contributed to a rising tide of insurgency against the US-led forces. Additionally, Iraq was plunged into bloody internecine violence as various gangs, ethnic and religious groups settled scores or fought for geopolitical supremacy. All this contributed to the accumulated misery of the Iraqi people that had resulted from a devastating war with Iran in the 1980s, the first Gulf War in 1991 and years of cruel and debilitating sanctions. The post-2003 scene was described variously as the "Iraq holocaust" and "a mess" that had returned Iraq to a "pre-industrial age" (Dyer 2007; Polya 2007a; Rihani 2004).

This chapter maps some consequences of the Iraq war in terms of its impact on civilians. Given the nature of the conflict, it was not always easy to distinguish between combatants and non-combatants. Certainly, the data on the dead and injured – derived largely from NGO sources – rarely separated civilians from non-civilians, combatants from non-combatants. In general terms, such data could be regarded only as broad indicators of the extent of civilian death and injury. Before looking briefly at some of these figures it is worth considering the way in which a key US strategy – the so-called US troop 'surge' of 2007 – was talked about by US military and political chiefs, if only to provide some useful insights into how the question of civilian casualties was addressed.

A web of illusions

For the US military and political leadership, the troop surge of 2007 came to symbolise hope in the face of carnage and destruction. Yet despite some notable successes resulting from this strategy, it also revealed the illusory and self-serving nature of US policy in Iraq. Prior to the surge the US military had become bogged down in bloody, urban warfare with a determined and increasingly well-resourced enemy. The death toll of US troops began to rise at an alarming rate and the White House was faced with growing public opposition to the conflict. The President's popularity began to head south. Damaging comparisons were being drawn between Iraq and Vietnam and the prospect of the unthinkable – defeat – set off the alarm bells in Washington. President Bush came out fighting on 10 January 2007 in a live TV address to the American people in which he admitted that:

> The situation in Iraq is unacceptable to the American people – and it is unacceptable to me. Our troops in Iraq have fought bravely. They have done everything we have asked them to do. Where mistakes have been made, the responsibility rests with me ... It is clear that we need to change our strategy in Iraq.

Having consulted with the bi-partisan Iraq Study Group, members of Congress, military commanders and diplomats, President Bush announced that:

> I've committed more than 20,000 additional American troops to Iraq. The vast majority of them – five brigades – will be deployed to Baghdad. These troops will work alongside Iraqi units and be embedded in their formations. Our troops will have a well-defined mission: to help Iraqis clear and secure neighbourhoods, to help them protect the local population, and to help ensure that the Iraqi forces left behind are capable of providing the security that Baghdad needs (Bush 2007).

After an initial period of heightened violence, especially in Baghdad, there were signs that the levels of insurgency had diminished to a point where US commander, General David Petraeus, and President Bush could assert with some confidence that Iraq had gained a semblance of peace and stability thanks to the surge (Al Jazeera 2008). We were told by military and political leaders that the 'rate' of killing had decreased significantly and that Iraq had become a more stable place, even in the major conurbations (Reuters 2007; CNN 2008). This, of course, turned out to be perverse reasoning given that even though the death rate among Iraqi civilians had indeed declined (that is, in the latter half of 2007 after an initial six months of terrible bloodletting), it did so only to a rate that vastly exceeded the pre-invasion death rate.

Publicly at least, the US military was reluctant about undertaking civilian body counts. The precedent was set in early 2002 during the Afghan campaign when General Tommy Franks of the US Central Command (who later headed all operations in the Middle East) said, rather dismissively, that "we don't do body counts" (cited in Epstein 2003) which, perhaps unintentionally, became a symbol of US indifference both to Afghani and Iraqi fatalities. The reality, however, was that the US military occasionally undertook body counts – the resulting data of which they sought to suppress – even though their methods of data collection were highly suspect (Whitaker 2004). The military bean-counters (located mainly in the bowels of the Pentagon) were reluctant to count dead civilians because they asserted that local conditions and customs did not allow for such a process or that in the heat of combat it was not possible to count the dead. Perhaps not surprisingly, the question of civilian body counts became an "invisible issue" as far as the US was concerned (Epstein & Mathews 2005; Thomas 2003). When it came to the question of those injured in hostilities, our reluctant empiricists devoted even less of their collective energies. Had they done so – using the crude yardstick of three casualties to every fatality – the injury rate among Iraqi civilians would have been (circa mid-2007) in the region of three and a half million. To complicate matters, many of the civilian deaths acknowledged by the US military were attributed to criminal acts committed by thugs, paramilitary gunmen, 'terrorists' or 'insurgents' (Jackson 2003; Krane 2006) or put down simply to accidents, lapses or general aberration. Speculation was rife in this area.

When figures were drawn from NGOs and respected academics who conducted most of the more meaningful empirical studies, US leaders tended to rely on the lower estimates. This exercise in strategic ignorance revealed a desperate attempt to screen out the full and ugly realities of war. It was also designed to massage public opinion and to deflect attention from the awkward spectre of the mounting dead and injured. A similar attempt to deflect public awareness of the dead also applied to US troop fatalities. Until recently (in fact, under the Obama presidency) public disclosures of the US dead were discouraged and photographs of flag-draped coffins banned altogether. US troops in Iraq were made up largely of young conscripts pulled from the more marginalised sections of the community, mainly young blacks and Hispanics, the unemployed and thousands of 'illegal' migrant 'volunteers' signed up on the promise of a green card and more (Hil 2005). This rag-bag army, a sort of latter day colonial expeditionary force, suffered terribly at the hands of its opponents.

Over four thousand US troops died from 2003 up to March 2009 – a daunting figure that fuelled even greater international opposition to the war and placed great pressure on the increasingly unpopular US Presidency. But the deaths of US troops, as we shall see, paled in significance against the number of innocent Iraqis who have perished since 2003. We will never know the precise scale of death and injury to the Iraqi people or how many of the population of twenty-five million may – or may not – survive the next few years. The continuing lack of a functional health service, enduring violence, unexploded munitions and depleted uranium, and the sheer scale of the existential tragedy are enough to guarantee that death (already a widespread occurrence) will continue at an alarming rate.[1]

Body count: no place to hide

By controlling the outflow of news and regulating the activities of 'embedded' journalists, the US military was able to present – officially at least – a sanitised view of the conflict. Even in the midst of the most brutal assaults, as in Fallujah in late 2004, the 'news' was either partial (mainly obtained through independent Iraqi journalists) or non-

---

1 For a comprehensive review of the scale of death and destruction in Iraq from 2003 onwards, see Hil & Wilson 2008.

existent. Yet faced with copious news coverage on the Internet, Iraqi blogs, and Arab TV news, it was becoming increasingly obvious that there were competing versions of reality when it came to the question of Iraqi body counts. The Pentagon went into full propaganda mode in early 2007 following President Bush's announcement of a troop surge that would finally subdue Iraqi insurgency – even though for Al Qaeda the prospect of more bloodletting of US soldiers was precisely what they wanted. Falling troop and civilian death rates coupled with elections eighteen months earlier had, according to President Bush, demonstrated the gradual restoration of democracy in Iraq. There were also signs that the Iraqi government was taking the necessary steps to achieve lasting political change and that the embryonic Iraqi army was reaching the awkward early threshold of autonomy. There was more good news: some militias announced a ceasefire or, lured by financial inducements, turned their guns on Al Qaeda instead of the US military. The rate of kidnappings (a major business enterprise in Iraq) and car bombings both declined from mid-2007 onwards. This development, publicised by British NGO Iraq Body Count (2008), was seized upon by the Pentagon and the Western corporate media as evidence of the success of the troop surge (RNIF Alternative News 2007). (Iraq Body Count was the favoured source of the US military since their comparatively modest estimates of the dead were based only on verified news reports.) In early 2008 parts of Baghdad even had their street lights turned on for the first time in five years – a sign that stability had begun to emerge. This was in fact a false dawn.

Unfortunately for the US leadership, the illusion of growing peace and stability in Iraq took several unwanted turns for the worse in 2008. On 24 March the four-thousandth US soldier was killed. On the same day sixty Iraqi civilians lost their lives, roadside bombs exploded in several parts of the country and there were shootings in a Baghdad market and a number of mortar shells landed square in the Green Zone (Colvin 2008). This was too much like the pre-surge bad old days.

The illusion was further shattered on the fifth anniversary of the 2003 invasion. The International Committee of the Red Cross (2008) issued a report which concluded:

> Five years after the outbreak of the war in Iraq, the humanitarian situation in most of the country remains amongst the most critical in the world. Because of the conflict millions of Iraqis have insufficient access to clean water, sanitation and health care ... The current crisis is exacerbated by the lasting effects of previous armed conflicts and years of economic sanctions ... Civilians continue to be killed in the hostilities. The injured often do not receive adequate medical care.

In April, Amnesty International (2008) issued a report entitled *Carnage and despair: Iraq five years on* in which they described Iraq as "one of the most dangerous countries in the world, with hundreds of Iraqi civilians killed every month". This was not good news for the White House. But surely there were signs that the Iraqi government was introducing the required changes to make Iraq a better, safer and more secure place? Unfortunately not, according to the Iraq Study Group (cited in Wright 2008), who described political changes in Iraq as "slow, halting and superficial".

Of all the unwelcome news perhaps the most harmful (or irritating) to the US leadership was the growing public concern over the number of Iraqi civilian deaths. The first major bout of unwanted news came early in 2006 when a team of respected US epidemiologists from Johns Hopkins University in Baltimore estimated that the death toll since the 2003 invasion was 654,965 (Roberts 2006). The derivative figure of 650,000 stood as a major benchmark in the grim catalogue of death in Iraq. It was a figure that could not easily be swept aside, despite all the attempts by Downing Street and the White House to do so. The UK Ministry of Defence Scientific Adviser, Sir Roy Anderson, noted – much to the embarrassment of his own government – that the methods used by the researchers to come up with this figure were "robust ... close to best practice" (cited in Bennett Jones 2007). Although there was considerable debate over the methods used by the Johns Hopkins researchers, the fact remained that the civilian death toll was considerably higher than most reports had hitherto indicated (Ahmed & Jamail 2008). The study served to further undermine the data on which the US leadership and Western media had relied; namely, that emanating from Iraq Body Count (IBC). The methods used by IBC and its subsequent modest figures of Iraqi civilian dead were now exposed, at best, as extremely limited (Pilger 2008).

But things got even worse for the leaders of the 'coalition of the willing'. In September 2007, a well-respected British polling company, ORB (2007), put the figure of Iraqi dead at 1,220,580. Others, like Australian researcher Gideon Polya (2007b), also stated that more than a million civilians had died. Alarmingly, if these figures were correct, then more Iraqi people had died since 2003 than all the combined fatalities during the Hussein period of government. The figure was higher than the genocide committed in Rwanda in 1994 and approached the death toll in the Cambodian killing fields (Holland 2007).

If the number of Iraqi dead made for grim reading, the news was equally depressing when it came to the actual financial and other costs of the conflict. The Nobel prize winning economist, Joseph Stiglitz, and academic Linda Bilmes (2008), put the financial costs of the war – factored in terms of hardware, maintenance, replacement and the costs of welfare and health care for the over 100,000 injured US military personnel – at around $3 trillion. In mid-2007, according to Stiglitz and Bilmes, the war was costing about $12 billion per month. Significant by any standard, this figure takes on even greater proportions when 'hidden' or 'opportunity' costs of the conflict are taken into account. The biggest impact has been on the world's poor and needy – including those in the heartlands of coalition countries. Back in the comparatively cheap days of 2004, the Portland Independent Media Centre (2004) estimated that the amount of money expended by the US on the Iraq invasion and occupation could have done a lot to alleviate the plight of the world's poor – a point that resonates in light of the recent global financial crisis to which Stiglitz and Bilmes say the Iraq war contributed.

In effect, the invasion of Iraq was a war mounted against a sovereign nation which, as it turned out, posed no direct threat to the US, Britain or Australia, *and* a proxy war against the world's poor. Arguably, had the funds expended on the war been devoted to addressing disease, hunger and poverty, millions of lives could have been spared and peace may have come to Iraq and other parts of the globe. As it turned out, the war resulted in death and destruction on a biblical scale, contributed to a failing world economy (with all its current disastrous consequences), involved incalculable hidden costs, and produced greater instability in the Middle East and beyond (Dyer 2007). Moreover, the US, Britain and Australia – leading 'multinational' partners in the assault on Iraq in 2003 – have become pariahs in the Arab world.

What is to be done?

Armed with knowledge of the injurious scale of the Iraq conflict, the task facing academics and the many non-government organisations who have chronicled the death and destruction in Iraq is to continue with this invaluable work. The more pressing issues are to do with what can be done to assist the Iraqi people to rebuild their shattered lives and how the instigators of the invasion in 2003 can be held to account. Professor Stuart Rees from the Sydney Peace Foundation at the University of Sydney has called for monetary compensation to be given to the Iraqi nation, the return of its assets, rebuilding of its economy in a similar way to the Marshall Plan, the installation of a truth and reconciliation commission, and the formation of an Arabic peace-keeping force once the coalition forces have left Iraq (Rees 2008). These are sensible proposals to which one might add the need for a form of democratic governance that represents the interests of all Iraqi people and not the interests of foreign powers or particular factions and groupings within Iraq. It might also be suggested that the stripping of Iraq's economy – in contravention of the Geneva Convention – be subject to some sort of trenchant legal action. But there are other questions around justice and accountability that need to be addressed: when and how might the political, military and corporate leaders who presided over an illegal and unjust invasion be held to account before an international forum? Are the existing international legal institutions anywhere strong enough (or sufficiently uncoupled from the interests of the US) to enact such a process? If not, what system of reform can be put in place to ensure that this happens?

And reform is certainly needed. The calls for 'never again' are made more in hope than reality given that history has endlessly repeated itself since both world wars. Perhaps the best we can hope for when naked self-interest and duplicity raise their heads is that the international legal institutions are strong enough to uphold international law. The evidence relating to the invasion of Iraq is that they are not. Unilateralism should be a crime in a world increasingly cognisant of its vital interconnections. One of the most eloquent and impassioned commentaries on the invasion of Iraq was made by the 2005 winner of the Nobel Prize for Literature, Harold Pinter. His words have been quoted often, mainly I suspect because they so eloquently capture the passion that people feel when they talk about the invasion of Iraq. It is for this reason that his words are worth citing again:

> The invasion of Iraq was a bandit act, an act of blatant state terrorism, demonstrating absolute contempt for the concept of international law. The invasion was an arbitrary military action inspired by a series of lies upon lies and gross manipulation of the media and therefore of the public; an act intended to consolidate American military and economic control of the Middle East masquerading – as a last resort – all other justifications having failed to justify themselves – as liberation. A formidable assertion of military force responsible for the death and mutilation of thousands and thousands of innocent people.
>
> We have brought torture, cluster bombs, depleted uranium, innumerable acts of random murder, misery, degradation and death to the Iraqi people and call it 'bringing freedom and democracy to the Middle East'.
>
> How many people do you have to kill before you qualify to be described as a mass murderer and a war criminal? One hundred thousand? More than enough, I would have thought. Therefore it is just that Bush and Blair be arraigned before the International Criminal Court of Justice (Pinter 2005).

Pinter might have added John Howard, Alexander Downer and Robert Hill to the list of political leaders to be charged under international law for war crimes. Others could include the many coalition politicians who gave support to the invasion, military leaders and possibly corporate chiefs who profited from this bloody conflict.

In seeking to build peace throughout the world it is necessary to have in place a system of international law and legal institutions to ensure that leaders of powerful states cannot unilaterally invade sovereign nations. It is with this optimism that we might view the actions taken by the International Criminal Court against the President Omar Hassan al-Bashir of Sudan and former Serbian leader, Radovan Karadzic. Though such cases are difficult to prosecute, this should not deter the pursuit of justice for wrongs done against innocent people.

The Iraqi people – like other oppressed peoples around the world – deserve the full protection of international law. In common with the people of Cambodia, they may require a process of healing that includes the application of legal principles in a case where a great harm has been done to innocent people.

References

Ahmed, A. & Jamail, D. (2008). IRAQ: death toll 'above highest estimates'. *IPS*, 2 June. Retrieved from ipsnews.net/news.asp?idnews=42618.

Al Jazeera (2008). Bush says Iraq surge is 'working'. 10 March. Retrieved from english.aljazeera.net/NR/exeres/7A676D32-86DF-4AE7-B35B-E7C82553F2F6.htm.

Amnesty International (2008). *Carnage and despair: Iraq five years on*. Retrieved from www.amnesty.org/en/news-and-updates/report/carnage-and-despair-iraq-20080317.

Bamford, J. (2004). *A pretext for war: 9/11, Iraq, and the abuse of America's intelligence agencies*. New York: Doubleday.

Bennett Jones, O. (2007). Lancet was right – shock. *New Statesman*, 2 April. Retrieved from www.newstatesman.com/society/2007/04/iraq-death-toll-lancet-survey.

Bush, G.W. (2007). Address to the nation on the troop surge in Iraq. Retrieved from lpau.zemgo.com/LandingZemgo.aspx?LpID=9985&PartnerID=adsmrkt&sourceid=000IoZ0rCRYR2hCnSh8f7JJXRt000000&sid=9174&ce_cid=000IoZ0rCRYR2hCnSh8f7JJXRt000000.

Chandrasekaran, R. (2008). *Imperial life in the emerald city: inside Baghdad's green zone*. London: Bloomsbury.

CNN (2008). Pentagon: violence down in Iraq since 'surge'. *CNN.com/world*, 23 June. Retrieved from edition.cnn.com/2008/WORLD/meast/06/23/iraq.security/index.html.

Cockburn, P. (2006). *The occupation, war and resistance in Iraq.* London: Verso.

Colvin, R. (2008). US death toll in Iraq hits 4,000. *The Independent*, 24 March. Retrieved from www.independent.co.uk/news/world/middle-east/us-deathtoll-in-iraq-hits-4000-800017.html.

Dyer, G. (2007). *The mess they made: the Middle East after Iraq.* Melbourne: Scribe.

Epstein, E. (2003). Success in Afghan war hard to gauge – U.S. reluctance to produce body counts makes proving enemy's destruction difficult. *San Francisco Chronicle*, 23 March, Retrieved from www.globalsecurity.org/org/news/2002/020323-attack01.htm.

Epstein, J. & Mathews, B. (2005). Tally of civilian deaths depends on who's counting – definitive estimates difficult to obtain. *San Francisco Chronicle*, 12 May. Retrieved from www.sfgate.com/cgi-bin/article.cgi?file=/c/a/2005/05/12/MNG9UCML2E59.DTL.

Fisk, R. (2003). Meet the new Iraqi strongman: Paul Bremer; thugs in business suits. *Counterpunch*, 9 September. Retrieved from www.counterpunch.org/fisk09092003.html.

Frame, T. (2004). *Living by the sword? The ethics of armed intervention.* Sydney: UNSW Press.

Hil, R. (2005). Life lottery: US military targets poor Hispanics for frontline service in Iraq. *New Internationalist*, May.

Hil, R. (2008). Civil society, public protest and the invasion of Iraq. *Social Alternatives,* 27(1): 29–33.

Hil, R. & Wilson, P. (2008). *Dead bodies don't count: the forgotten costs of the Iraq conflict.* Brisbane: Zeus Publications.

Holland, J. (2007). *Iraq death toll rivals Rwanda genocide, Cambodian killing fields.* AlterNet, 17 September. Retrieved from www.alternet.org/story/62728/.

International Committee of the Red Cross (ICRC) (2008). *Iraq: no let-up in the humanitarian crisis.* Geneva, Switzerland. Retrieved from www.icrc.org/web/eng/siteeng0.nsf/htmlall/iraq-report-170308/$file/ICRC-Iraq-report-0308-eng.pdf.

Iraq Body Count (2008). *Civilian deaths from violence 2007.* 1 January. Retrieved from www.iraqbodycount.org/analysis/numbers/2007/.

Jackson, D. (2003). US evades blame for Iraqi deaths. *The Boston Globe*, 12 December. Retrieved from www.boston.com/news/globe/editorial_opinion/oped/articles/2003/12/12/us_evades_blame_for_iraqi_deaths?mode=PF .

Krane, J. (2006). Solid figures missing on total death toll. *The Seattle Times*, 19 March. Retrieved from seattletimes.nwsource.com/html/nationworld/2002874731_iraqdead19.html.

Kristol, W. (n.d.). *Project for the New American Century*, website, www.newamericancentury.org/.

Opinion Research Business (ORB) (2007). *September 2007 – more than 1,000,000 Iraqis murdered.* Retrieved from www.opinion.co.uk/Newsroom_details.aspx?NewsId=78.

Pilger, J. (2008). Iraq body count: a shame becoming shameful. *Media Lens*, 10 April. Retrieved from www.medialens.org/alerts/06/060410_iraq_body_count.php.

Pinter, H. (2005). Art, truth and politics. Nobel lecture, 7 December. Retrieved from nobelprize.org/nobel_prizes/literature/laureates/2005/pinter-lecture-e.html.

Polya, G. (2007a). US Iraqi Holocaust and one million excess deaths. *Countercurrents.org*, 7 February. Retrieved from www.countercurrents.org/iraq-polya070207.htm.

Polya, G. (2007b). Body count: global avoidable mortality since 1950. Weblog, 3 June, globalbodycount.blogspot.com/.

Portland Independent Media Center (2004). *The financial costs of war.* Retrieved from portland.indymedia.org/en/2003/07/267510.shtml.

Rampton, S. & Stauber, J. (2003). *The uses of propaganda in Bush's war on Iraq.* Sydney: Hodder Headline Australia.

Rees, S. (2008). Bring on the bricklayers without borders. *New Matilda*, 25 April. Retrieved from www.newmatilda.com.

Reuters (2007). Petraeus says Iraq 'surge' working: paper. 31 August. Retrieved from www.reuters.com/article/topNews/idUSSYD20420070831.

Rihani, S. (2004). Iraq's holocaust. *Global Complexity*, 30 August. Retrieved from www.globalcomplexity.org/Iraq'sHolocaust.htm.

RNIF Alternative News (2007). Iraq body count: BBC and other mainstream media use misleading figures. Retrieved from rinf.com/alt-news/media-news/iraq-body-count-bbc-and-other-mainstream-media-use-misleading-figures/1408/.

Sands, P. (2005). *Lawless world: America and the making and breaking of global rules.* London: Penguin.

Stiglitz, J. & Bilmes, L. (2008). *The three trillion dollar war: the true cost of the Iraq conflict.* New York: W. W. Norton.

Thomas, H. (2003). Who's counting the dead in Iraq? *Miami Herald*, 5 September, (cited in CommonGround.org). Retrieved from www.commondreams.org/views03/0905-04.htm.

Whitaker, R. (2004). Pentagon suppresses details of civilian casualties, says expert. CommonDreams.org, 31 October. Retrieved from www.commondreams.org/headlines04/1031-01.htm.

Willis, G. (2004). What is a just war? *New York Review of Books.* Retrieved from www.nybooks.com/articles/article-preview?article_id=17560.

Wright, R. (2008). Iraq report details political hurdles and future options. *The Washington Post*, 6 April. Retrieved from www.washingtonpost.com/wp-dyn/content/story/2008/04/05/ST2008040502204.html.

3

The human and environmental costs of the Iraq and other wars

Sue Wareham

The human and environmental costs of war are so far-reaching that a full examination of them would produce countless volumes. Humanitarian disasters, enormous loss of life, far greater numbers maimed or injured, psychological trauma, destruction of essential services, human rights abuses, floods of refugees and crippling economic cost are all a part of war's legacy. Increasingly, as climatic and other environmental threats loom large, contributions of war and its preparation to environmental destruction must also feature prominently in our examination of the price we pay for a heavily-militarised world.

It is important to emphasise that the 'environmental' impacts of war are very much a cost that we humans pay. We have only one planet to provide our food, water, shelter and all our other needs and pleasures. As we destroy it, we destroy our future. In his foreword to *The true cost of conflict* (Cranna 1994), the Rt Hon Lord Judd of Portsea wrote:

> It is an extraordinary fact that so much of the work done to raise the quality of life of our fellow human beings is frustrated and negated by conflict. Every major famine in recent years has taken place in a war zone. In my six years as director of Oxfam, our priority was, as it is now, long term development. But over 50 per cent of Oxfam's work was in areas of

conflict. In Africa, 70 per cent of our work was war-related, and remains so today.

The statistics about modern warfare and its impact on civilians are chilling. Although most wars in the 18th and 19th centuries caused relatively few civilian casualties, in World War I, approximately 14% of the dead were civilians, in World War II approximately 67% and in the 1990s an estimated 90% of deaths in wars were civilians (Levy & Sidel 1997, p. 33). However, not only did the percentage of civilian deaths increase greatly during the last century, but the degree of destruction caused in the process increased. Since World War II, there have been more munitions expended for every enemy soldier killed than previously. Iraq provides a tragic illustration of practically every one of war's costs. They were all predicted before the current war began in 2003. Some of the effects of this and other wars will be examined in this chapter.

Human security costs

Mortality estimates for the 2003 war in Iraq vary widely. This war, like all wars, was sold to us on morally righteous grounds, so the spin-doctors have worked hard in an effort to present a sanitised picture. However, as discussed in the previous chapter, in October 2006 the eminent medical journal *The Lancet* published a study (Burnham et al. 2006) from Johns Hopkins Bloomberg School of Public Health in Baltimore, which estimated that the number of conflict-related deaths from the start of the war up until July 2006, above and beyond the deaths that would usually have occurred, was 655,000 and 92% of those deaths were due to direct violence. In quick response, and in total ignorance of the way in which such studies are conducted, political leaders in the US, the UK and Australia ridiculed the report. Journalist Richard Horton (2007) reports that, in the UK at least, government ministers had been advised by their own scientists in the Ministry of Defence that the research was accurate and reliable.

A more recent estimate of the Iraqi death toll was made by the US group Just Foreign Policy in August 2007, and that estimate was over 999,000 – practically one million Iraqi deaths due to the invasion and its consequences. According to Iraq Coalition Casualty Count (2009), the occupying forces have suffered heavy losses also. Over 4,200 US soldiers have been killed (up to February 2009).

Deaths are, of course, only the tip of the iceberg of the humanitarian effects of war. They are far out-numbered by maiming, other physical injuries, and severe psychological disturbances, all of which perpetuate the suffering and drain scarce resources from postwar economies. While physical injuries are the most visible, it is psychological injury that is often more incapacitating, both for civilians and military personnel. Medact, the UK affiliate of International Physicians for the Prevention of Nuclear War, in its 2008 report, *Rehabilitation under fire: health care in Iraq 2003-7* (Medact 2008), emphasised the profound impact that mental health problems will have on the country's future.

For the occupying forces also, rates of psychological trauma are alarming. A study by Milliken, Auchterlonie and Hodge (2007) of more than 88,000 Iraqi war veterans, published in the *Journal of the American Medical Association*, found high rates of psychological disorders, alcohol abuse and interpersonal conflict. The psychological impacts of this war on coalition soldiers and their communities are compounded by the fact that the troops were told they were going as liberators. Instead they were attacked by Iraqis as occupiers.

Essential services are generally disrupted in times of war, sometimes by deliberate targeting. Iraq's health care system suffers grave problems, including destruction of facilities, the exodus of thousands of doctors, university teachers and other workers, the abduction, killing and torture of doctors, and deliberate attacks on hospitals and clinics (Ismael 2006).

The briefing paper 'Rising to the humanitarian challenge in Iraq' (Oxfam International 2007) estimated that almost a third of the Iraqi population was in need of emergency aid. It added that the 'brain drain' had seen about 40% of Iraq's teachers, doctors, engineers and other professionals leave the country while unemployment affected over 50% of the remaining population. Moreover, clean water, sanitation and electricity services were drastically reduced, even compared to 2003 levels after over a decade of crippling economic sanctions.

Medact's 2007 report on health care in Iraq since 2003, cited above, drew attention to some of the deliberate policy decisions that increased the scale of the humanitarian disaster in Iraq. The report stated that: 1) health facilities were not protected during or after the invasion and only the ministries of oil and of the interior had military protection; 2) during the attacks on Fallujah in 2004, no humanitarian corridor was provided, as vividly detailed by Donna Mulhearn in chapter ten of this book, and elsewhere checkpoints prevented access to health facilities; 3) the enforced sacking of Ba'ath party members removed many senior health experts; 4) advice from the UN, WHO and other sources with relevant experience in health care was largely ignored particularly by the Pentagon, who had a virtual monopoly on post-invasion reconstruction, including in health care; and, 5) well-functioning systems such as the Oil-for-food distribution network for food and medicines was undermined by the US drive for privatisation in everything.

Perhaps the greatest of humanity's failures in relation to warfare is the failure to protect children. Children growing up in war zones, where they have witnessed or even taken part in extreme acts of violence, can develop chronic and very disabling psychological disorders. This is particularly so when children are forced into militias. UNICEF (2007) estimates there are 300,000 child soldiers worldwide. Children are also vulnerable to many of war's deprivations. In particular, disruption of the supply of food and clean water leads to high mortality from outbreaks of infectious illnesses. In the1991 Gulf War, the US destroyed 85–90% of Iraq's electrical generating capacity in the full knowledge that it would lead to an inability to run water treatment plants, resulting in the spread of infectious illnesses that would kill children in disproportionate numbers (Nagy 2004, p. 139).

In July 2007, UNICEF reported that the plight of Iraqi children was deteriorating (Jordans 2007). This was attributed partly to the fact that the government-funded food rations that had been provided by Saddam Hussein's regime in response to the economic sanctions were no longer available. Also fear of violence prevented mothers from accessing health care for their children. Fear prevents many Iraqi children from attending school. Oxfam's 2007 report, cited above, stated that 92% of Iraqi children suffered learning difficulties mostly because of the pervasive climate of fear, and that more than 800,000 children had dropped out of school.

Throughout history, women have often been regarded as the property of the victors in war, and subject to rape and capture as sex slaves. Mass rape is also used to humiliate and to destroy social cohesion in the enemy. However, sexual crimes against women have generally received much less attention than other war crimes. The scale of rape in war often remains hidden for many years, an example being the 100,000-200,000 'comfort women', mostly Korean, used by the Japanese in World War II. In the war in Bosnia, many thousands of women were raped, partly in an attempt to cause panic, terror and Muslim retreat from territories claimed by the Serbs.

Even refugee camps do not necessarily provide safe haven for women, as they can also be a centre for sexual exploitation, which is rarely documented or punished. In societies where women and girls are disadvantaged in access to education, crippling military expenditures, even without the outbreak of war, reduce even further their chances of attending school, and thus confine them to a life of illiteracy with all its consequences.

Many who can flee a war-ravaged region do so. In Iraq, the refugee crisis is the biggest in the Middle East for sixty years. Over four million Iraqis – a sixth of the population – have been displaced, either internally or into neighbouring countries, especially Syria and Jordan, placing enormous strain on those countries (Goldenberg 2007; Gavlak 2007). Many of the refugees have limited access to health care in their host country, and three quarters are women and children under twelve, who are economically vulnerable.

However, disrupting a nation's identity is not only evident in displacement of peoples in wartime. A nation's identity also derives from its history and cultural records. For this reason, cultural heritage is often destroyed during warfare in an attempt to humiliate and to destroy the sense of uniqueness and pride that binds and strengthens nations and groups, or simply in shameful and chilling ignorance of cultural values. In Iraq, such wanton destruction was nothing short of catastrophic, described by Chalmers Johnson as 'the smash of civilisations'. In his August 2008 essay of the same title, Johnson refers to:

the indifference – even the glee – shown by [US Defense Secretary] Rumsfeld and his generals toward the looting on April 11 and 12, 2003, of the National Museum in Baghdad, and the burning on April 14 of the National Library and Archives as well as the Library of Korans at the Ministry of Religious Endowments.

Approximately 15,000 items were stolen from the museum's showcases, including clay tablets containing cuneiform writing and other inscriptions going back to the earliest discoveries of writing itself. These crimes in the region known as 'the cradle of civilisation' were not just against the people of Iraq. They represent an irreplaceable loss for the whole of humanity.

Economic and environmental costs

According to the Stockholm International Peace Research Institute (SIPRI 2008), global military expenditures for 2007 reached US$1.339 trillion as mentioned in the previous chapter. The economic cost of the war in Iraq has been estimated by Joseph Stiglitz, former chief economist at the World Bank, and Linda Bilmes from Harvard University, at $3 trillion. This estimate takes into account the cost of providing health care and other services to the veterans over coming decades. By comparison, the World Bank (2004) estimates that the amount of additional foreign aid needed per year to achieve the Millennium Development Goals (MDGs) by 2015 is $40–60 billion. The MDGs would provide the eradication of extreme hunger and poverty, universal primary education, a reduction of child mortality, the empowerment of women, environmental sustainability and other essential goals. Quite apart from the need to achieve the MDGs for their own sake, erasing the sources of so much human misery and despair would do far more to reduce the threat of terrorism than any amount of military spending.

Wars do not occur in an ecological vacuum. Whether on land, at sea, or in the air, the footprint of war and its preparation is heavy. The final frontier, space, is also being militarised, including through US missile defence systems, with largely unknown environmental consequences. War-related damage to our natural environment occurs in a large number of ways. Destruction of wildlife habitats is the most obvious, but most of war's environmental costs are hidden.

The movement of tens or hundreds of thousands of troops, especially to distant shores, with all their fighting equipment and means of survival, including medical and other essential infrastructure, is an extremely fuel-intensive undertaking. And that's even before the fighting starts. Modern fighting machines burn fuel at rates that make most civilian usage pale by comparison. Two examples illustrate the point. The Worldwatch Institute estimated in 1991 that a B-52 bomber flying for one hour uses 13,671 litres of fuel (Renner 1991). The current model Abrams tank in service in Iraq moves less than one mile for every gallon of fuel used – that means more than 235 litres per 100 kilometres (Turse 2008). The US military is the biggest purchaser of oil in the world, using a total of approximately 350,000 barrels (fifty-five million litres) of fuel each day (Karbuz 2008; Hobbs 2008). Michael Klare (2007), Professor of Peace and World Security Studies at Hampshire College, Massachusetts, states that the US uses more oil annually for combat operations in Iraq, Afghanistan and the whole South West Asian region than the whole of the nation of Bangladesh with its 150 million people.[1]

A study ordered by the Pentagon and released in 2007 stated that the military in Iraq and Afghanistan are using sixteen times more fuel per soldier than in World War II, more than half of all cargo transported is fuel (Bender 2007). In Australia, the Department of Defence (establishments plus operations) uses approximately 65% of total Australian Government energy usage (Australian Greenhouse Office 2007). Fossil fuel supplies are not only depleted by the machinery of war, but they may also be deliberately targeted. In 1991, Saddam Hussein's forces unleashed an ecological disaster by igniting 600 oil wells across Kuwait as they retreated, and spilling four million barrels of oil into the Persian Gulf (Lash 2002). There was massive damage to hundreds of kilometres of coastline, including mudflats, marine life, migratory and local birds, coral reefs, mangroves and sea-grass beds. Soot, gases and chemicals spread as far as the Himalayas. The heavy reliance of the world's militaries on oil, and their significant contributions to its disappearance, complete a self-perpetuating cycle of destruction.

---

1 Klare calculates approximately 3.5 million gallons (13.2 million litres) every day.

Military exercises and wars themselves leave behind an array of toxic chemicals, unexploded ordnance and environmental time-bombs. Heavy metals, polychlorinated biphenyls (PCBs), acids, alkalis and explosives pollute many thousands of former military sites around the world, with impacts on human and environmental health. Subic Bay in the Philippines is one example, where tons of waste were dumped in the bay when the US Navy had a base there. In 2007, thousands of tons of dumped World War II munitions were fished up by trawlers in the Baltic, which was a dumping ground for Hitler's armies. They include chemical weapons which were developed by Hitler's scientists but never used. As the casings rust, phosgene and mustard gas are leaching into the food chain, rendering many former fishing spots unusable (Hall 2007).

In Vietnam, dioxin from the approximately eighty million litres of Agent Orange that were sprayed over the environment between 1962 and 1971 takes a very heavy toll still and probably will for generations to come. The Vietnamese Government estimates that 500,000 children have been born with birth defects caused by Agent Orange, although research to confirm this is lacking (Laurance 2006). The US Government has evaded both the necessary research and compensation for the victims. Large areas of the country remain contaminated. Landmines, cluster bombs and other unexploded ordnance present major problems also for communities trying to recover from war, making a mockery of the word 'ceasefire'. Tens of millions of landmines in dozens of countries render large areas of land uninhabitable, and maim and kill civilians long after hostilities have ceased. After the 2006 Israeli attacks on Lebanon, over a million unexploded cluster bombs remained. Their removal is slow, painstaking and dangerous.

A particularly iniquitous and toxic legacy of war that poses an ever-increasing threat to Pacific Island countries is the slowly corroding World War II shipwrecks, mostly Japanese and US, and numbering over 1000, on the ocean floor (Christie 2002). In Truk Lagoon in the Federated States of Micronesia, 200,000 tonnes of warship were sunk in an area just over sixty kilometres across. In 2001, up to 91,000 litres of fuel from the oil tanker USS Mississinewa, which sunk in 1944, spilled into Ulithi Lagoon in Micronesia, preventing the islanders from fishing for their food. The South Pacific Regional Environment Program (SPREP), which is attempting to avert further and even more disastrous oil leaks, faces major obstacles in engaging the flag state nations in the clean-up, in part because the wrecks are regarded as war graves. The economic cost also is formidable. SPREP has thus far catalogued fifty oil tankers among the wrecks. Closer to Australia, the oil tanker USS Neosho was sunk in 1942 during the Battle of the Coral Sea, and lies just 200 nautical miles off the Great Barrier Reef.

Depleted uranium (DU) is a by-product of the uranium enrichment process. (It is 'depleted' of the more fissile uranium, U-235, that is used in nuclear reactors.) It has both chemical toxicity and low-level radioactivity, and a half-life (time taken for half the radioactivity to decay) of 4.5 billion years. Where DU is used therefore, low-level radioactivity will remain indefinitely. DU is favoured in weaponry because of its density and armour-piercing ability. Being a waste product, it is also plentiful and cheap. It ignites on penetration (for example, of a tank) and the particles which form can carry tens of kilometres in the wind. DU has been used extensively in some recent wars, in Iraq, Kosovo, Bosnia and almost certainly Afghanistan. In Iraq in 1991, approximately 300 tons were used by US forces. UN statistics show a seven-fold increase in cancer in southern Iraq, where DU was used most heavily, since 1991. As with Agent Orange in Vietnam, studies to demonstrate (or disprove) the alleged link have not yet been carried out. The use of DU was condemned by the UN Human Rights Subcommittee in 1996.

War's environmental impact is not simply of theoretical interest for Australia. Beginning in 2001, Australia has hosted the biennial Talisman Sabre (TS) joint US-Australia military exercises, held primarily at the Shoalwater Bay Military Training Area in Queensland, adjacent to the Great Barrier Reef. TS 2007 involved 26,100 troops, with exercises (including live fire) being conducted on land, at sea and in the air. Tanks and other heavy equipment traversed the landscape. TS 2009 was on a similar scale. Nuclear powered vessels are involved, with the attendant risks of accident and leakage of radioactive waste. (In February 2009, British and French nuclear submarines collided deep in the Atlantic Ocean.)

The marine environment is also threatened by the use of sonar. In 2007, the International Whaling Commission warned Australia that sonar used in the exercises could seriously injure or kill whales. In the same year, the US Navy claimed an exemption from the Marine Mammal Protection Act, resulting in the right to conduct whatever tests it chose for the following two years (*The Canberra Times* 2008). Shoalwater Bay is the very same region where Minister for the Environment Peter Garrett rejected, on environmental grounds, a 2008 proposal for a rail line and coal port. The Minister found the proposal to be "clearly unacceptable" under the *Environment Protection and Biodiversity Conservation Act 1999*. He referred to "the internationally recognised Shoalwater and Corio Bay Ramsar wetlands and the high wilderness value of Shoalwater which is acknowledged in its Commonwealth Heritage listing", and said that "the impacts would destroy the ecological integrity of the area" (Garrett 2008). The Defence Department justified its environmental credentials in October 2008, when appearing before a Senate inquiry reviewing the *Environment Protection and Biodiversity Conservation Act*. The department claimed that it should be exempt from environmental protection laws, stating that the laws caused delays, and that it wanted a fast-track process (Beeby 2008).

Nuclear costs

Nuclear weapons demand particular attention. They represent mankind's ultimate means of self-destruction and our ultimate confrontation with the natural environment. The purpose of these weapons is wholesale destruction on a massive scale. No other single human creation has such potential for harm either in the short term or over geological timeframes. The weapons that destroyed Hiroshima and Nagasaki were approximately fifteen and twenty-one kilotons respectively (a kiloton being 1,000 tons of TNT equivalent). The two cities were destroyed and, by the end of 1945, over 200,000 people had died as a result of these two weapons. Nuclear weapons built since then have been up to many megatons (million tons of TNT equivalent). The largest US and Soviet nuclear tests were, respectively, a fifteen megaton test (codenamed Bravo) in 1954, and a fifty megaton test in 1961 (Norris & Kristensen 2003, p. 72).

In 1996, the International Court of Justice, the world's highest legal authority, delivered its landmark ruling on the general illegality of these weapons, stating: "[t]he destructive power of nuclear weapons cannot be contained in either space or time. They have the potential to destroy all civilisation and the entire ecosystem of the planet." Even the existence of these terrifying weapons is a situation beyond humanity's capacity to manage. Human error and miscalculation guarantee that eventually they will be used. Human fear guarantees that they will be used as political tools. And equity dictates that as long as some nations keep them, other nations will claim the right to do so. Fear of the existence of nuclear weapons helped boost support for the invasion of Iraq, and plays a similar role in creating an aggressive posture towards Iran. In other words, the weapons themselves are incompatible with peace. Despite no nuclear weapon having been detonated in warfare since 1945, the development of these weapons since then has caused permanent and severe human and environmental damage.

Approximately 1,900 nuclear tests have been conducted, of which just over 500 were in the atmosphere, underwater or in space and the remaining 1,400 were underground. Radioisotopes produced by nuclear tests, such as carbon-14, caesium-137, strontium-90 and plutonium-239 (half-lives 5,730 years, 30 years, 28 years and 24,400 years respectively), pose risks to current and future generations by ingestion, inhalation and external radiation. Test sites around the world remain contaminated, including the Maralinga site in South Australia.

In 1991, International Physicians for the Prevention of Nuclear War and the Institute for Energy and Environmental Research (IPPNW & IEER) published *Radioactive heaven and earth: the health and environmental effects of nuclear weapons testing in, on and above the earth*. This study estimated that the radiation exposure from fallout delivered to the world's population until the year 2000 would cause 430,000 cancer deaths, and that exposure to long-lived carbon-14 (integrated over infinity) would result in a total of 2.4 million human cancer deaths. The study concluded that "[m]any aspects of nuclear weapons testing have been characterised by a disregard, sometimes wilful, of public health and environment". In the US, in 1997, the National Cancer Institute revealed that atmospheric tests at the Nevada site resulted in significant contamination of the nation's milk supply with iodine-131, with estimates of 11,000 to 212,000 excess thyroid cancers as a result (Simon, Bouville & Land 2006).

Evidence has accumulated of major health, safety and environmental problems at nuclear weapons complexes around the world. This is most apparent in the two nations that are responsible for approximately 96% of the world's nuclear weapons, the USA and Russia. In the US, the task of dealing with the toxic and radioactive legacy of 50 years of nuclear weapons production is said to be the most technologically challenging and costly public works project ever conceived. The US Department of Energy has estimated that minimal remediation of the nuclear weapons complex will cost $230 billion over seventy-five years. Even at this level of expenditure, many sites and buildings will remain out-of-bounds for human access for the foreseeable future (Kimball 1997).

At Hanford, the former plutonium production complex in Washington State, approximately 800 billion litres of low-level liquid radioactive waste were discharged directly into the soil over a fifty-year period. Groundwater at Hanford has been heavily contaminated with radioactive and toxic substances. High-level radioactive waste at Hanford is stored in 177 underground tanks, seventy of which have leaked (Makhijani et al. 1995, p. 28).

In Russia, the situation is probably worse than in the US. Vast quantities of radioactive waste, including nuclear reactors, from Soviet and Russian nuclear-powered ships and submarines were dumped into the Pacific and Arctic Oceans. The vast Mayak complex in the eastern Ural Mountains (also called Chelyabinsk-65, or Kyshtym) is the largest of the former Soviet Union's three plutonium production centres. The highly contaminated site lies on a region of interconnecting lakes, marshes and waterways at the headwaters of the Techa River. Between 1948 and 1956 radioactive waste from the Mayak nuclear complex was poured straight into the river, the source of drinking water for many villages. Cesium, strontium and other liquid radioactive waste that had been dumped was detected in the Arctic Ocean nearly 1,000 miles away. The waste discharge point at Lake Karachay in the Ural Mountains remains so radioactive that a person standing there would receive a lethal dose of radiation in less than one hour (Makhijani, Hu & Yih 1995, p. 2).

Recent studies have reminded us of the reality of 'nuclear winter' scenarios put forward in the 1980s. It is estimated that the use of just 100 Hiroshima-sized weapons in urban areas, for example in a war between India and Pakistan where each side used fifty weapons, could cause severe global climatic consequences (Robock et al. 2006). Fires ignited would release copious amounts of light-absorbing smoke and debris into the upper atmosphere, causing persistent surface cooling even a decade later. In such a scenario, there would be decreases in growing seasons in many of the most important grain producing parts of the world, resulting in severe reductions in food production. It is not the solution we need for global warming. A scenario of this magnitude could lead to a total global death toll of one billion people from starvation alone, major epidemics of infectious disease, and immense potential for further war and civil conflict (Helfand 2007).

Not a single country, anywhere, has in place a satisfactory long-term solution to the problem of nuclear waste. Unless a solution is developed, all future generations of humans will inherit this problem. In the US alone, the burden includes approximately 15,000 tons of high level waste from nuclear weapons production (MacFarlane 2006). All the current storage sites are intended as temporary sites, but there is nowhere else for the waste to go. The proposed Yucca Mountain site has experienced prolonged delays, despite many billions of dollars of research. In February 2009, President Obama essentially eliminated further funding for the site.

Where to from here?

War is not a solution to any of humanity's pressing problems. Whether our main agenda is addressing climate change, salvaging the natural environment, eradicating poverty, upholding human rights, or securing our cities from terrorist attack, war must be de-legitimised and opposed. It has proven itself counter-productive to all these tasks. Even preparations for war place an unsustainable burden on our human, environmental, technological and economic resources. Simply put, war is a costly distraction for humanity.

Campaigns for climate change action, environmental remediation, social justice and human rights should recognise the negative impact of war and its preparation on achieving these goals. The peace movement has natural allies in all these spheres.

According to the Defence Department's own 2008 policy discussion paper, Australia faces no threat of attack by another country (Department of Defence 2008, p. 28). Yet Australia is spending $62 million per day on our military forces and on weapons systems that consume vast quantities of fossil fuel, threaten our neighbours and perpetuate futile wars. At the same time, many sectors of our society suffer chronic shortages of funds. Resources for housing, health care, education, environmental rescue efforts, and a host of other critical needs are found wanting, while Australian governments proudly announce increasing military expenditures.

In the region and globally, the needs are even more pressing and yet Australia still fails to meet the modest UN target of 0.7% GDP as overseas development aid. Globally, military budgets represent a theft from the poor of their basic means of survival. Australia's bloated military spending also represents lost opportunities to promote good relations in our region and beyond, and ultimately undermines our security.

For the world's most destructive weapons, nuclear weapons, abolition is long overdue. ICAN, the International Campaign to Abolish Nuclear Weapons, was initiated in Australia and is gathering speed globally. Its goal is a Nuclear Weapons Convention to ban these instruments of terror. The website www.icanw.org invites the participation of all Australians.

The dignity of humankind is trampled mercilessly by wars that feed on lies and are conducted with brutality. While brutality towards our fellow humans has always been in the nature of warfare, our technological prowess now extends that brutality to our natural environment. As we allow military juggernauts to destroy and pollute the land, sea and air that give us life, we destroy our only means of surviving as a species. It is not simply a matter of human dignity, although that is also essential. Opposing the war machine is now a matter of human survival.

References

Australian Greenhouse Office (2007). *Energy use in the Australian government's operations 2005–2006*, Department of the Environment and Water Resources. Retrieved from www.environment.gov.au/settlements/government/eego/energyuse/pubs/2005.pdf.

Beeby, R. (2008). Defence wants free rein on training. *The Canberra Times*, 10 October. Retrieved from www.canberratimes.com.au/news/local/news/general/defence-wants-free-rein-on-training/1330065.aspx.

Bender, B. (2007). Pentagon study says oil reliance strains military. *The Boston Globe*, 1 May. Retrieved from www.boston.com/news/nation/washington/articles/2007/05/01/pentagon_study_says_oil_reliance_strains_military/.

Burnham, G., Lafta, R., Doocy, S. & Roberts, L. (2006). Mortality after the 2003 invasion of Iraq: a cross-sectional cluster sample survey. *The Lancet*, 368(9545): 1421–28. Retrieved from www.thelancet.com.

Christie, M. (2002). World War Two wrecks haunt Pacific with oil spills. *Planet Ark*, 4 November. Retrieved from www.planetark.org/dailynewsstory.cfm/newsid/18431/story.htm.

Cranna, M. (Ed.) (1994). *The true cost of conflict: seven recent wars and their effects on society*. London: Earthscan Publications.

Department of Defence (2008). *Key questions for defence in the 21st century: a defence policy discussion paper*, Defence Publishing Service. Retrieved from www.defence.gov.au/whitepaper/docs/Public_Discussion_Paper.pdf.

Garrett, P. (Minister for the Environment, Heritage and the Arts) (2008). *Minister says no to Shoalwater Bay rail and port*. Media release, 5 September. Retrieved from www.petergarrett.com.au/614.aspx.

Gavlak, D. (2007). War-scarred Iraqis face health burdens in foreign lands. *Bulletin of the World Health Organisation* 85(9): 649–732. Retrieved from www.who.int/bulletin/volumes/85/9/07-030907/en/index.html.

Goldenberg, S. (2007). Refugees in their own land: 2m Iraqis forced to flee their homes. *The Guardian*, 20 September. Retrieved from www.guardian.co.uk/world/2007/sep/20/iraq.suzannegoldenberg.

Hall, A. (2007). Dumped German wartime munitions are a 'timebomb in the Baltic'. *The Scotsman*, 3 April. Retrieved from news.scotsman.com/worldwarii/Dumped-German-wartime-munitions-are.3273185.jp.

Helfand, I. (2007). An assessment of the extent of projected global famine resulting from limited, regional nuclear war. Presented at the Nuclear Weapons: The Final Pandemic Conference, London, 3–4 October. Retrieved from www.ippnw.org/News/Reports/HelfandFaminePaper.pdf.

Hobbs, S. (2008). The new oils of war. *The Diplomat*, 27 August. Retrieved from www.the-diplomat.com/article.aspx?aeid=8683.

Horton, R. (2007). A monstrous war crime. *The Guardian*, 28 March. Retrieved from www.guardian.co.uk/commentisfree/2007/mar/28/iraq.freedomofinformation.

IPPNW & IEER (1991). *Radioactive heaven and earth: the health and environmental effects of nuclear weapons testing in, on and above the earth.* New York: Apex Press; London: Zed Books.

Iraq Coalition Casualty Count (2009). *Iraq Coalition Casualty Count.* Retrieved from icasualties.org/Iraq/index.aspx.

Ismael, S. (2006). Doctors for Iraq. Lecture, Australian National University, 22 May.

Jordans, F. (2007). UN: Iraqi children worse off. *Associated Press*, 16 July. Retrieved from the University of Sydney, Factiva document APRS000020070716e37g00dcy.

Just Foreign Policy (2007). The estimate explained. Retrieved from www.justforeignpolicy.org/iraq/counterexplanation.html.

Karbuz, S. (2006). The US military oil consumption. *Sohbet Karbuz: on U.S. military energy consumption, geopolitics, peak oil, oil market, twisted truths.* 25 February, weblog. Retrieved from karbuz.blogspot.com/2006/02/us-military-oil-consumption.html.

Kimball, D. (1997). US Dept. of Energy's nuclear weapons complex. *Physicians for social responsibility*. Retrieved from www.psr.org/site/PageServer?pagename=security_legacy_military_weaponscomplex.

Klare, M. (2007). The Pentagon vs Peak Oil. *tomdispatch.com*, 14 June. Retrieved from www.tomdispatch.com/post/174810/michael_klare_the_pentagon_as_global_gas_guzzler.

Lash, J. (2002). Beware an ecological catastrophe in Iraq. *International Herald Tribune*, 13 December. Retrieved from unitedforpeace.rdsecure.org/article.php?id=375.

Laurance, J. (2006). Vietnam's poisonous legacy. *The Canberra Times*, 9 April. Retrieved from University of Sydney, Factiva document CANBTZ0020060408e2490002j.

Levy, B.S. & Sidel, V.W. (Eds) (1997). *War and public health*. New York: Oxford University Press.

MacFarlane, A. (2006). Stuck on a solution. *Bulletin of the Atomic Scientists*, 62(3): 46–52.

Makhijani, A., Hu, H. & Yih, K. (Eds) (1995). *Nuclear wastelands: a global guide to nuclear weapons production and its health and environmental effects*. Cambridge MA: MIT Press.

Makhijani, A., Ruttenber, A.J., Kennedy, E. & Clapp, R. (1995). "Nuclear Wastelands: Nuclear Weapons Production Worldwide and its Environmental and Health Effects" in *Medicine and Global Survival*, 2(1): 26–34.

Medact (2008). *Rehabilitation under fire: health care in Iraq 2003-7*. London, UK. Retrieved from www.ippnw.org/ResourceLibrary/RehabilitationUnderFire.pdf.

Milliken, C.S., Auchterlonie, J.L. & Hodge, C.W. (2007). Longitudinal assessment of mental health problems among active and reserve component soldiers returning from the Iraq war. *Journal of the American Medical Association*, 298(18): 1023–32.

Nagy, T. (2004). Safeguarding 'our' American children by saving 'their' Iraqi children: Gandhian transformation of the DIA's genocide planning, assessment and cover-up documents. In T.Y. Ismael & W.W.

Haddad (Eds). *Iraq: the human cost of history* (p. 139). London: Pluto Press.

Norris, R.S. & Kristensen, H.M. (2003). Nuclear pursuits. *Bulletin of the Atomic Scientists*, 59(5): 71–2.

Oxfam International (2007). Rising to the humanitarian challenge in Iraq. Briefing Paper, July. Retrieved from www.oxfam.org/sites/www.oxfam.org/files/Rising%20to%20the%20humanitarian%20challenge%20in%20Iraq.pdf.

Renner, M. (1991). Assessing the military's war on the environment. *State of the World 1991*, Worldwatch Institute.

Robock, A., Oman, L., Stenchikov, G.L., Toon, O.B., Bardeen, C. & Turco, R.P. (2006). Climatic consequences of regional nuclear conflicts. *Atmospheric Chemistry and Physics Discussions*, 6(6): 11817–43.

Simon, S.L., Bouville, A. & Land, C.E. (2006). Fallout from nuclear weapons tests and cancer risks. *American Scientist Online*, 94(1), January–February.

Stockholm International Peace Research Institute (SIPRI) (2008). *SIPRI Yearbook 2008*. Retrieved from yearbook2008.sipri.org/.

The Canberra Times (2008). Songs of the Deep. 26 October, Book review of David Rothenberg's *Thousand mile song: whale music in a sea of sound*, Basic Books.

The World Bank (2004). *The costs of attaining the Millennium Development Goals*. Retrieved from www.worldbank.org/html/extdr/mdgassessment.pdf.

Turse, N. (2008). The Military-Petroleum Complex. *Foreign Policy in Focus*, 24 March. Retrieved from www.fpif.org/fpiftxt/5097.

UNICEF (2007). *Child protection from violence, exploitation and abuse: children in conflict and emergencies*. 27 November. Retrieved from www.unicef.org/protection/index_armedconflict.html.

4
Spectacles of honour: barbarism within civilised reactions to public killings[1]

Sandra Phelps

Both human dignity and human survival are lost in the Du'a Khalil story. This chapter explores people's responses to the brutal killing of Du'a Khalil in 2007 in Northern Iraq. Du'a was killed in a public stoning. She was dragged to the market place in her home village Bashiqa where hundreds of men, including police officers, gathered to participate in her killing. Many stood by and watched, others filmed the slaying on their cell phones and some hurled the boulders that would finally crush the life from her young body (Mahmoud 2007). The scene depicts a brutality and disregard for human life that is indeed barbaric. A scene which leaves many viewers with the question: how can this violence happen in today's world?

My interest here lies in examining the way in which the world – Kurds, Iraqis and others – constructs and evaluates this painful display of femininity, brutality, life and death. In my research I examined the texts of online reactions to this murder. I read through the many hundreds of responses posted on sites such as CNN and YouTube as well as the many thousands of signatures offered to the International Campaign Against Killing and Stoning of Women in Kurdistan.[2] The online campaign is

---

1 First published in *The International Journal of the Humanities*, 6(5): 141–46.
2 Honour crimes in Iraq are certainly not rare occurrences. Although exact numbers are difficult to determine, my estimate is that there are around two to four of these killings every day in the Kurdistan region alone depending on one's

the primary source referred to in this paper. Signatures to this campaign are most often named rather than anonymous and they generally identify their affiliated organisations.³

The spectacle of Du'aas death provides a platform for expressions of not only deep sympathy and horror but also the stage for voicing systemic intolerance and violence in our world. Reactions to her story articulate deep national and ethnic shame, a plethora of dichotomised stereotypes (East/West, male/female, Islam/Christian, Islam/Ezidi,⁴ Kurd/Arab, innocence/guilt), and contain disturbing expressions of increasing religious and ethnic intolerance and hatred towards perceived others.⁵ Perhaps most paradoxical given the aggressive occupation in Iraq by US allied forces and security companies which have proliferated so much needless violence and fear, are reactions to this tragedy underpinned by a belief in cultural divisions between the civilised and the barbaric. It is the barbarism inherent within the public and fatal stoning of Du'a that occupies the forefront of international criticism regarding this sexual-

---

definition of what constitutes an honour crime (see Hosali 2003 and Yifat 2007 for a discussion of such definitions). With such figures one has to conclude that along with a sense of shame there is a concurrent sanction for the slaying of women for honour related reasons – albeit in less barbaric ways. The failure to prosecute in the vast majority of these murders is further testimony to this sanctioned form of violence.

3 Organisations range from universities, UN institutions, Amnesty International, peace and legal organisations to trade labour movements. It is difficult to establish whether these are representative of general opinion. However, the campaign signatures (with the exception of a few clearly provocative comments) are the comments of signatories who take the issue very seriously and are not random responses posted anonymously in cyberspace. There are more than 16000 signatures to date. The campaign is organised by Houzan Mahmoud with the aim of pressing the Kurdistan Regional Government to protect and ensure the rights of women. I am greatly indebted to Mahmoud for her efforts and support.

4 Du'a was a member of the Ezidi faith, one of the oldest religions in the Middle East. Since Zoroastrian times, Ezidi have suffered determined religious attacks against them. It is a closed religion of around 700,000 (Haji 2007).

5 I am not suggesting that all responses to this scene are reactions of violence, but rather that this reaction is evident in a significantly large number of the responses and that violence surfaces within the viewer in the encounter with this brutal killing.

ised brutality. It is barbarism that saturates every angle of this tragedy. And it is barbarism that evokes the uncanny repetition of barbaric violence within specific versions of civilised humanity.

While these reactions give voice to various seemingly conflicting perspectives, in some ways the polarised responses of horror, sadness and sympathy on the one hand and anger and hatred on the other meet in the vociferous condemnation of Du'aas killers. Moreover, many of these polarised identifications unite in the presumption of the right not simply to judge but also to execute the sentence upon those who committed this heinous crime.[6] The Internet has become the stage for the mass performance of ruling that extends its verdict further than the village of Bashiqa to all of Iraq and the Middle East. As a spectator, the trauma of violence inherent in the witnessing of Du'aas death does not stop at the moment of her final breath but continues in the narratives of reaction. The violence itself extends beyond the geography of Bashiqa to all those geographies that connect. The violence emerges from the disparate voices across the world.[7]

What makes Du'aas murder central to this research is that the crime was captured on mobile phone video, expediently posted on the Internet and internationally covered on major television broadcasts and Internet sites. This was not planned coverage by established news teams, but rather, spontaneously captured by the very perpetrators at the scene. Furthermore, this is not the same as the everyday sectarian violence occurring in Iraq and depicted on regular news broadcasts. This is a violence directed not towards the enemy – not Sunni against Shiite or

---

6 While punishment provides a clear and necessary message that the killing of women like this is unacceptable it may also mean that the killing of women is obfuscated, reinvented and takes on new forms. For instance we are now witnessing a disturbing rise in female suicides, generally by means of self-immolation in the Kurdistan region of Iraq. Many suspect that these suicides are in fact also honour murders (Mohammad 2008).

7 Honour killing can not be reduced to geography, to religion, to patriarchy or to tradition. These are all key dimensions that may support this system of violence but they do not individually stand alone. Rather, they make up a system of violence that perpetuates violence throughout our world. For further discussion on honour related crimes, see Al-Khayyat 1990; Ahmed 1992; Mojab 2002; and King 2008.

Ezidi against Muslim – but towards the self, the family. "Honour killing is a tragedy in which fathers and brothers kill their most beloved, their daughters and sisters" (Mojab 2002). It is an erstwhile secret violence that now through the conduit of Du'aas death has burst into every corner of the globe to disturb all of our civilised sensitivities. The dissemination of this spectacle is a chance contingent upon the historical, technological and regional circumstances that permit this.

Over a year later, one can still log on and watch Du'a as she dies. In witnessing that moment one can almost feel her final breath. Du'aas murder and dying moments are a public spectacle open to the whole world. In some ways it is possible for us to own, to possess, her death. This theatre of horror, this pornographic spectacle of brutality, is ours. Whether we like it or not this violence belongs to us all and as witnesses to this slaying we too are implicated in the consequences.

In his most recent book, *Violence*, Slavoj Zizek (2008) addresses the question of whether the spectator could continue to go on as usual after being witness to such a scene of brutality. He concludes:

> Yes but only if he or she were able somehow to forget – in an act which suspended symbolic efficiency – what had been witnessed. This forgetting entails a gesture of what is called fetishist disavowal: 'I know but I don't want to know that I know, so I don't know.' I know it, but I refuse to fully assume the consequences of this knowledge, so that I can continue acting as if I don't know (pp. 45–46).

Reading the postings from those who have watched Du'aas death gives support to Zizek's observation. There is an overwhelming disavowal inherent within the comments of the witnesses and a general disbelief that this kind of killing can continue in the 21st century. There is open dismissal of the immediate and overwhelming Kurdish reproach of such an act[8] and there is a subsequent disavowal of the humanity of Du'aas

---

8 Apparent in this analysis is the immediate reaction from Kurdish people. Three central themes emerge in this regard. The first is a deep sense of urgency to stop honour-related crimes and to respect Kurdish women's right to live without this kind of fear in their lives. The second related theme is anger towards politicians and people in positions of power for failing to prevent such crimes. The final

killers and by extension all Kurdish men, sometimes women too – all Ezidi, Arab, Muslim, indeed all Middle Eastern people.

In a violent process of racialised othering, there are several calls for the extermination of all Ezidis, Muslims and Arabs, charges of devil-worshipping and Kurds are constructed as primitive, prehistoric, monkeys, dogs, rats, animals; the very humanity of the villagers is brought into question. This disavowal of the humanity of the Other functions to put a distance between the civilised viewer and the barbaric Other that allows the viewer to refuse to fully assume the consequences of the knowledge that this type of brutality is indeed human. The distance placed between the viewer and the scene is more than merely geographical. The distance created is epistemological, moral and religious; the distance is human. I know but don't want to know. I saw these humans killing this young woman with stones but I don't want to believe that they are humans. They are humans but they are not a part of civilised humanity. This action is not of the civilised world, it belongs to the barbaric Other; it is inhumane – not human. There is a consequent disavowal of the violence within the self in these expressions; the civilised subject must disavow all memory of internally repressed barbarism in order to maintain a civil self-image diametrically opposed to the barbaric. Du'a thus becomes the threshold between the civilised and barbaric worlds and her feminine body functions as the buffer zone that constitutes the divisions between them.

In his analysis of today's liberal tolerance towards Others, Zizek makes the observation that this tolerance comes hand in hand with the demand that the Other keeps his distance. "My duty to be tolerant towards the Other effectively means that I should not get too close to him, intrude on his space. In other words, I should respect his intolerance of

---

theme, and perhaps the most ambiguous regarding Kurdish responses, reveals a deep sense of shame for being Kurdish. In the words of Kurdish people: "These are the days I am feeling shame to be a man and moreover a Kurdish man. Damn this barbaric act! Damn this genocide committed against my sisters, mothers and fellow humans." "My God I just don't have any words to describe this ... But the only thing that I can say is that for the first time in my whole life I hate myself being Kurdish!" (International Campaign Against Killing and Stoning of Women in Kurdistan).

my over-proximity" (2008, p. 35). According to this point of view, we can tolerate the Other only when a safe distance between the self and the Other is maintained: a distance that permits the tolerance of difference on the one hand and avoidance of an encounter on the other. The public broadcasting of Du'aas killing transgressed this safety zone between the civilised self and the barbaric Other. Her murder and the brutal Other emerged as too close, at a dangerous proximity to the self. In the civilised encounter with such a barbaric act of cruelty, the viewing subject comes face-to-face with such violence and from the words of many viewers it is apparent that this encounter itself evokes a traumatic and pathological response:

> "They should be burned aliveeee"
>
> "all those who have stoned her, their heads should be cut off."
>
> "These men that kill young girls should be hung from lamp posts, Animals."
>
> "cruel and satanic people did this work. Down with them."
>
> "shoot the men and send the women here."
>
> "Personally I believe no man should be left to leave the outbounds of that country, for life, in order not to carry away the evil that binds them for centuries."
>
> "not only should the women be killed but the men as well they are just parasites to humanity."
>
> "The fact that similar events occurred all the time gives justification for the Western invasion of Iraq. Modern Western Values are better for Iraq than the cold and dark, unfree and jealous, values they have"
>
> "They should castrate every single male that believes in this barbaric honour killing so that he won't have an opportunity to father children so he can murder them"
>
> "we must kill all those killers"
>
> "The murderers of ths young woman are Sick and should be put down like you would a rabid dog"
>
> "beat them all to death – slowly. I pray for that."

[sic] (Quotations from individual signatures to the online International Campaign Against Killing and Stoning of Women in Kurdistan 2007–2008).[9]

"Maybe the civilized world needs to ban together and just rid the planet of these scumbags"

"i think this is a good reason for killing many of those Iraqi fucks"

"Fucking animals. Someone should drop a bomb over thoose countries down there. Thoose people makes me SICK!"

"i wished that saddam killed all with that chemical weapon but they lived just like rats."

"bomb whole iraq and iran and afghanistan so we finally can live without these monkey shit's"

[sic] (Quotations from individual online responses to CNN Internet video coverage of Du'aas murder).[10]

How can sense be made of these statements? What right or reason is there to respond to the barbaric with violence, to murderers with execution? How many people should be killed, how many killers should be killed? How is it possible to reconcile absolute disgust and repulsion at such an act of violence with the desire to find a humane solution? Will the pathologisation of an entire culture, be that ethnic, religious, gendered or geographical, provide a solution to the humanitarian quest to bring about justice and equality for women – to ensure the basic human right to live without fear? When reading through the many comments such as those above it is evident that we must rethink our responses to violence evoked through moral outrage. As Zizek advises, if we are to think critically about violence "we should learn to step back, to disentangle ourselves from the fascinating lures of this directly visible 'subjective violence' performed by a clearly identifiable agent" (2008, p. 1). Responses of moral outrage at subjective, clearly visible violence

---

9 The above responses are from people who signed the petition against the killing and stoning of women in Kurdistan. They all identify their organisations and give authorship to their comments.

10 The above five responses are posted on CNN websites and are anonymous.

are not only unsuccessful in addressing violence in its less visible forms or in recognising the conditions through which this may emerge, but moral outrage also serves to obfuscate the violence within our response – within our civilised selves. From the responses it is evident that these reactions of outrage do not function outside the discourse of violent barbarism to which they seek to separate. Indeed these responses reveal an inherent participation within this same system of violence.[11]

The spectacle of Du'aas murder provides an opportunity to think about violence in a serious way that demands we look beneath the surface of what Zizek calls 'subjective violence'. The violent racism voiced within so many of the online narratives of outrage reveals a pathological condition brought to light through the encounter with Du'a. Within this encounter the civilised subject is presented with the opportunity of analysis and analysis reveals that the outrage to the barbaric act itself rests upon a repressed barbarism that exists deep within the civilised self. Violence within the civilised subject resurfaces in the struggle to respond to the traumatic event and this struggle brings to the surface a range of persistent racist and deadly attitudes towards the Middle East.

The underlying barbarism within these condemning responses to the barbaric may well be viewed as mere emotive reactions to such horror, to the trauma of being a spectator to such an unthinkable act. However, it is possible that these comments reflect more insidious problems than this. For one, reading these texts reveals that indeed there is a flip side

---

11 We are not disconnected from this violence and for those of us who occupy the geographical territories where honour crimes are more prevalent, there is a responsibility to recognise that our very occupation of space makes us directly involved in the political and social structures that condone such violations. We must evaluate our positions and the price we pay, or are paid, to occupy such landscapes. In this globalised world the responsibility for these inhuman attitudes and actions lies also with the multinational corporations and the international community in all its manifestations, who are complicit by investing in these environments and who have the economic and political firepower and influence to require change and to promote the protection of human rights. If global investors can take the responsibility to ensure the protection of archaeological sites and antiquities, and of the flora and fauna, they must also have responsibility for, and influence on, enhancing the lives of people. If the environment must be protected, then so should the people.

to civility, there is an underbelly to our claims of progressive humanity. Perhaps this is the stage in human progress that Norbert Elias discusses in his theorising of de-civilisation, in which he refers to evidence of regress, such as war, in our civilising process (1994, p. 106).

However, it is more useful to think of this encounter with the barbaric in terms of Freud's (1919) uncanny return of the repressed. It is the repressed barbarism – this underbelly of brutality – that confronts us when we come face-to-face with images such as this. The barbarism repressed by the demands to represent civilised humanity is not something that the subject has overcome through progressive cultural values that produce repulsion to such acts. Neither is this a stage in a civilising process wherein the civilised subject is suffering a temporary reversion in the long civilising process. Rather, it is more accurate to view these violent responses to barbarism as something hidden in the struggle to represent an image of civil subjectivity. The barbarism is that which is repressed within the civilised subject but simultaneously that which constantly threatens to reappear and incite trauma in the subject.

Freud stipulates that when confronted with the appearance of the uncanny, the subject is thrown into hysterical illness wherein the subject recites the same incoherent language connected to previous uncanny encounters. In the online signatures to the International Campaign Against Killing and Stoning of Women in Kurdistan, there is an undeniable repetition of certain words used to describe the feelings of anger, disgust, sadness and shame of the viewer: savage, vicious, brutal, heinous, monsters, cowards, uneducated, barbaric, inhumane, pathetic, prehistoric, medieval, madness, primitive, demonic, abhorrent, cold-blooded, obscene, stone aged, premeditated, slaughter, horrendous, deranged, sadistic, grotesque, unlawful, unfathomable, unpardonable, unspeakable, unforgivable, unthinkable, shame.

The most common repetitions of language used to respond to Du'a are the words barbaric and civilised.[12] These opposing terms are couched

---

12 In his etymology of 'uncanny', Freud shows how a word and its opposite contain the same meaning which hinges around the notion of home. Using the German words 'heimlich', and its opposite 'unheimlich', he shows that the uncanny contains ambivalent meanings which represent feelings of both comfort and fear, foreign and familiar. "Thus heimlich is a word the meaning of which develops

within assumptions of an obvious ethnic and geographical distinction between the East and West where the West is aligned with civility and the East with barbarism. These voices of condemnation are alarming. Not because they condemn Du'aas murder, but rather, because so many of these civilised testimonies of condemnation contain an inherent barbarism that is alarming – a barbarism that one observes when looking into the faces of the frenzied crowd participating at the scene of Du'aas death. Expressions of barbarism are both foreign and familiar to the civilised subject. The barbarism within the so-called civilised response demands that we give critical analysis to the imagined and arbitrary divisions between civil/barbaric and East/West. This violent response to brutality brings into question the innocence of the judge in this situation.

The repetitive hysterical babble within this uncanny encounter is evident in the incoherent narratives that extend verdict for the crime of Du'aas murder throughout the Middle East. The hysteria is further evident in the calls to rid the planet of these scumbags, the calls that refuse to acknowledge that people in Iraq may abhor such brutality or that people in Iraq may also be civilised subjects. Moreover, within the hysteric's response, the brutality of her murder serves to justify the presence of US allied forces in Iraq and the Anfal campaigns under the Saddam regime. At one extreme of this violence, the hysteria extends to calls for nuclear eradication of whole populations of humans and at the other to hang the murderers and rescue the women. The Ezidi of Bashiqa provides the civilised hysteric with the evidence for religious condemnation and racist disavowal. Time after time the online respondent evokes similarly incoherent language when referring to the civil goodness of Western geography where women of Iraq could find a haven and the good intentions of the civilised world, while simultaneously repressing any memory or testimony to the contrary. Repeatedly, the goodness of the civil subject is elevated through further pathologisation of the Iraqi culture.

This performance of outrage – of locating the imaginary civilised world on the high ground of morality – rests upon the condemning subject's

---

towards an ambivalence, until it finally coincides with its opposite, unheimlich" (Freud 1919, p. 377).

desire to legitimate and maintain its civilised self-image. Freud makes the point that the uncanny return of that which ought to remain hidden is connected to the recurrence of the repressed memories of that part of the subject. The uncanny "is in reality nothing new or foreign, but something familiar and old-established in the mind that has been estranged only by the process of repression" (1919, p. 394). The uncanny return of that which has been estranged thus evokes fear and neurosis in the subject. In the civilised encounter with the barbaric, the subject is thrown into a fear that they too may disintegrate into barbarism. If the barbarism repressed within the civilised self reappears in the encounter that transgresses safe distance then does this uncanny reappearance not call into question the civilised subject itself? This uncanny encounter with violence reconstitutes civil/barbaric divisions and reveals a barbaric and racist pathology at the heart of many of those that claim the civilised moral space. The screening of Du'aas brutal killing exposed civilisation's weakness, the repression of barbarism and the underlying and persistent fear that 'we' – the civilised world – too could fall into the chaos of barbarism. Violent responses to Du'aas murder may indeed bespeak this pathology of fear at the heart of the viewer. While elevating the goodness of civility, barbaric responses surface as confronting these narratives. The uncanny return of the barbaric within the self disrupts the fetishist disavowal of the repressed and reveals that a pathological condition motivates the moral response.

It is inaccurate to suggest that these online comments represent social opinion in its totality. Certainly, in regard to language of expression, there is a notable difference between the comments posted on CNN and YouTube websites and those signatures in support of the International Campaign Against Killing and Stoning of Women in Kurdistan. However, given that the signatures to the campaign are mostly authored, alongside the ontology of foreign occupation within Iraq at present and the persistent campaigns purporting to alter the political and social structure of some Middle Eastern countries such as Iraq, it is evident that little value is held towards existing forms of civil governance or civil society. These voices parallel an inherent disavowal in general for the civility that has long been a part of countries such as Iraq. Often accredited as the birthplace of civilisation, perceptions of Iraqi society are at present not positive. The brutal slayings of Du'a and many young women like her in the name of honour further perpetuate such negative impressions and unhelpful stereotypes. These killings must stop if we are to have a world that respects the human rights of all people; and all governments of the world, as well as corporations and individuals, must recognise the interconnectedness of the humanity of all people. Unthinkable and barbaric violations against women such as that suffered by Du'a continue every day throughout our world. Although it seems reasonable to argue that there is indeed no honour in honour killings, that this is indeed a barbaric act, it is more difficult to explicate our civilised responses to this brutality.

How then is it possible to respond to such a violation of humanity in a way that does not participate in this system of violence? What does it mean to respond from the position of civility? If this barbarism is a part of our humanity then given the same accident of birth, given the same life, would we not also participate in this killing? Is it possible for us to recognise that while there is an obvious barbaric underbelly to civility, the opposite might also be the case? That underneath the barbaric there may lie civility and that this civility might present opportunities to encourage equal respect for women and their rights to live without fear of being killed for being women.

References

Ahmed, L. (1992). *Women and gender in Islam: historical roots of a modern debate*. London: Yale University Press.

Al-Khayyat, S. (1990). *Honour and shame: women in modern Iraq*. London: Saqi Books.

Elias, N. (1994). *The civilizing process: sociogenetic and psychogenetic investigations*. Oxford, UK: Blackwell Publishers.

Freud, S. (1919). *The uncanny*. H. Haughton (Ed), D. McLintock (Trans). London: Penguin.

Haji, A. (2007). Lalish is the beginning of life. *Baita Lalish*. Erbil, Kurdistan: Kurdistan TV.

Hosali, S. (Ed.) (2003). Selected International Human Rights Materials Addressing 'Crimes of Honour'. London, UK: CIMEL/Interights. Retrieved from www.soas.ac.uk/honourcrimes/Mat_IHRM.pdf.

International Campaign Against Killing and Stoning of Women in Kurdistan (2007). Retrieved 26 April 2008, from www.petitiononline.com/kurdish/petition.html.

King, D. (2008). The personal is patrilineal: namus as sovereignty. *Identities: Global Studies in Culture and Power,* 15(3): 317–42.

Mahmoud, H. (2008). *Killing women, destroying Iraq.* Organisation of Women's Freedom in Iraq, 5 May. Retrieved May 2008, from www.equalityiniraq.com.

Mohammad, S. (2008). Surge of violence against women in Iraqi Kurdistan. *AFP News Brief List, 24 May.* Retrieved June 2008, from www.france24.com/en/20080524-surge-violence-against-women-iraqi-kurdistan?q=node/1924390//2.

Mojab, S. (2002). 'Honor killings': culture, politics and theory. *Middle East Women's Studies Review,* 17(1/2). Retrieved from www.amews.org/review/reviewarticles/mojabfinal.htm; last updated 15th November 2006.

Project on Strategies to Address 'Crimes of Honour'. Retrieved from www.soas.ac.uk/honourcrimes/Projectfinal.htm.

Yifat, S. (2007). Promising democracy, imposing theocracy: gender-based violence and the US war on Iraq. *MADRE: Demanding Human Rights for Women and Their Families Around the World.* Retrieved December 2007, from www.madre.org/index.php?s=9&b=24&p=86.

Zizek, S. (2008). *Violence.* London: Profile Books.

5

The US invasion and occupation of Iraq and the implications for the Middle East: instability and the unravelling of US hegemony

Noah Bassil

The US invasion and subsequent occupation of Iraq polarised notions of the barbaric other in opposition to the civilised self. The 9/11 attacks on New York and Washington in 2001 provided the neo-conservatives in the Bush administration with the pretext they needed to unleash the overwhelming force of US military power against Saddam Hussein's regime in Iraq. Beginning with Bush's declaration of an 'Axis of Evil' in January 2002, the neo-conservatives in the US government, with the aid of the powerful pro-Israeli lobby, a compliant media, and Bush's closest international 'friends', especially British Prime Minister Tony Blair, initiated a campaign to convince the world of the immediate threat that Iraq posed to world peace and the urgency of a pre-emptive war to remove Saddam Hussein. Despite concerted opposition from the vast majority of the members of the international community, the US and the 'coalition of the willing' (as the US allies became known) invaded Iraq on 20 March 2003. Five weeks later on 1 May, the US had deposed Saddam Hussein and George W. Bush landed on the US aircraft carrier, the *Abraham Lincoln*, to announce to the world 'mission accomplished' in Iraq.

George Bush's premature declaration aboard the USS *Abraham Lincoln* marked the apogee of the Bush Doctrine and possibly of the Bush presidency. From that moment on the repercussions of the ill-advised invasion of Iraq became increasingly apparent. It is now a cliché but while the US undoubtedly won the war in Iraq, they subsequently lost the 'peace'. Events in Iraq in the years since May 2003 have regularly been described by commentators of all political hues as a mistake, debacle, disaster, shambles and a catastrophe. While the killings in Iraq have diminished since the surge in late 2007, there is still an uneasy feeling amongst a number of Iraq watchers that another outbreak of strife is not all that far away as the precarious sectarian and political alliances that have maintained the uneasy peace begin to tear at the seams (Hanna 2009). Iraq's severe problems remain the foremost legacy of the US invasion and occupation, and even as the Obama administration aims to successfully rebuild the stability of Iraq to allow an orderly extraction of the military, the repercussions of the US invasion and occupation will take decades for Iraqis to overcome. However, while the deep problems facing Iraq are a major cause of concern, the US intervention has wider ramifications that stretch beyond the borders of Iraq affecting the entire Middle East.

There has been a shift in the balance of power in the Middle East as the newly constituted Iraq rejoined Middle Eastern politics after the lost decade of the 1990s. In some circles, Iraq is believed to connect Iran with the Shi'a communities located in Lebanon, Bahrain, Saudi Arabia and Jordan, thus forming a potentially destabilising Shi'a crescent under the control of the radical Islamist regime in Tehran. While Iran's danger to the stability of the Middle East has been characterised in sectarian terms, the real threat is not in a Shi'a revival or crescent but in a more worrying radicalisation of the Arab public. There is now a growing fear amongst the conservative monarchies of the Gulf and Jordan, as well as the pro-US bourgeois government in Egypt, of the increasingly widespread popularity of the alternative politics projected by Iran. The result has been an overreaction by conservative governments of the Middle East, led by Saudi Arabia and Israel, to Iran and Iranian allies in the region. A new bellicosity in the Middle East by Arab states towards Iran is illustrated by the Arab support for the Sunni insurgency during the sectarian strife which unfolded in Iraq and the feebleness of the Arab response to the deadly Israeli assault on Hezbollah in 2006. A new 'Cold

War' between conservative governments and revolutionary movements for change has been unleashed by the US invasion of Iraq and is fast permeating the politics of the Middle East.

A major casualty of the largely unpopular invasion of Iraq has been the further erosion of America's "considerable post-9/11 sympathies of the world, which had even extended to parts of the regime in Iran" (Robins 2008, p. 293). A stronger sense of the negative role the US plays in the region can be seen as one of the deepest of the legacies of US adventurism in Iraq. In turn, the weakening of the US has undermined the existing political and social order, and has strengthened the inclination of disaffected members of the diverse Middle Eastern societies to seek solace in alternative ideologies, especially those put forward by anti-'Western' Islamist movements. The long-term impact of the war in Iraq and increased Muslim radicalisation for the Middle East is reminiscent of the situation after the Islamist victory over the Soviet Union in Afghanistan in 1989. After the Soviet withdrawal from Afghanistan, the Middle East was left to deal with the tens of thousands of Arabs who returned from Afghanistan extremely ideologically radicalised from their experiences and highly trained in the art of terrorism. It took the 9/11 attacks in 2001 for the rest of the world to understand the implications of the war in Afghanistan but in the Middle East an understanding of the longer term impact of war on regional instability was comprehended much earlier.

The implications of the US invasion and occupation of Iraq has unleashed potentially conflicting forces in the Middle East. Iran's influence in the Middle Eastern region has experienced a resurgence in the aftermath of the US invasion of Iraq – the removal of Saddam Hussein and the installation of an Iranian-friendly government in Iraq facilitating Iran's reach westward. The disastrous democratisation campaign of the Bush government has only served to reinforce to people of the Middle East that the US is not the beacon for change that US self-representation would have the world believe. With the rise of Iran and the increasing sense of disillusion amongst people of the Middle East, the region is set for a major upheaval. The public in the Middle East has lost all faith in the US model and in the governments that have allied themselves to the US, instead increasingly preferring Iranian-style Islamism. The destruction of Iraq, witnessed on prime-time television across the Middle East, has only served to radicalise people and create further public discontent, leading to a view that the Middle East is a powder-keg just awaiting a spark to set it off.

The fall of Iraq and the reawakening of Iran

The most apparent repercussion of the US invasion has undoubtedly been the tragedy of Iraq itself. The Iraqi population have paid an incredibly high price for the regime change that brought a putative liberation to that long-suffering country. Other chapters in this book enumerate the cost in human lives and the destruction of vital infrastructure, the devastation of the fabric of social relations, and the continuing insecurity in post-Saddam Iraq. My task, without ignoring the human tragedy, is to concentrate on exploring the political implications of the transition that has taken place as a result of the US invasion of Iraq in the context of the wider Middle Eastern region. One such repercussion is that there are still two million Iraqi refugees in the neighbouring states of Syria and Jordan. The Iraqi refugees present an international humanitarian crisis that threatens the stability of Syria and Jordan, with flow-on implications for Iraq's other neighbours, particularly Turkey and Lebanon. Syria and Jordan are struggling to accommodate the bulk of the two million Iraqi refugees who have escaped the violence of their own country. This influx of people into Syria and Jordan seeking housing, employment and social services has created a huge strain on the fiscal and human resources of these poor states (International Crisis Group 2008). So far, both Syria and Jordan have successfully managed the thin line between their sense of duty to Arab solidarity by caring for the Iraqi refugees and the necessity of maintaining essential services to the national populous. However, in the face of the global economic downturn, this precarious balance has the potential to falter if an increase in international assistance and aid is not forthcoming, or if Iraqis fail to return home in significant numbers. As important as resolving this humanitarian crisis for the stability of the Middle East is the question of the increasingly threatening geopolitical tensions which have arisen from the US invasion of Iraq.

A number of authors have focused their discussion of the impact of the US invasion in terms of the reawakening of the Iranian influence in the Middle East and the emergence of a possible 'Shi'a crescent' (Cole 2006; Sirriyeh 2007; Takeh 2008). King Abdullah II articulated Arab government fears that the Shi'a, who form majorities in Iraq, Bahrain, and southern Lebanon, are now controlled by Iran and that this Shi'a alliance is stronger now than at anytime since the fall of the Fatimids almost a millennium ago.[1] Another view on the rise of Iranian influence across the region explains Iran's increased standing in the region as a result of Iran's leadership in opposing the US in Iraq, and Israel in Lebanon. It has been a shared sense of resentment towards US and Israeli policy that has brought Middle Eastern public opinion in line with Iranian regional geopolitics and not simply Shi'a identity.

Iran's support for the Sunni Palestinian movement Hamas is just one example of the cross-sectarian nature of power politics in the Middle East. The 2008/2009 Israeli assault on Hamas-controlled Gaza, which claimed the lives of more than 1000 Palestinian civilians including 300 children, demonstrated the extent that conservative Arab governments considered Hamas a creature of Iran, and to a lesser extent Iran's closest regional ally Syria. During the twenty-two day Israeli onslaught against Gaza, most Arab governments voiced concerns over the number of civilian casualties but showed little interest in supporting Hamas. The isolation of Hamas by the majority of Arab states during the Israeli assault on Gaza confirmed what many commentators had suspected regarding the existence of a schism in Middle Eastern politics between conservative Arab regimes led by Saudi Arabia and Egypt and an alliance of radical states and movements led by Iran and comprising Syria, Hezbollah and Hamas. As these events in Gaza have recently shown, the tensions between conservative Arab governments led by Saudi Arabia and Egypt, and Iran and its regional sub-national allies,

---

1 A summary of the position presented by King Abdullah II of Jordan in 2004. In that interview on MSNBC, Abdullah stated that: "it was a Shia-led Iraq that had a special relationship with Iran. And you look at the relationship with Syria, Hizballah, Lebanon, then we have this new crescent that appears that would be very destabilising for the Gulf countries and actually for the whole region" (MSNBC 2004).

especially Hezbollah in Lebanon and Hamas pose a real problem for regional stability (Telhami 2007, p. 108).

The perception that Iran is a threat to the stability of the Middle East is most apparent in the vocal nature of the recurring Middle Eastern opposition to Iran, summed up by the bellicosity of numerous Middle Eastern heads of state. Israeli President Shimon Peres, for example, described the current situation as a "collision between the Middle East, which is Sunni Arab, and the Iranian minority that seeks to take it over" (Haaretz 2009). Peres articulates the division that now exists in the regional politics of which Israel is a major actor within the anti-Iranian bloc. A more precise characterisation of the impending collision, which Peres speaks of, is between a largely entrenched authoritarian ruling elite perceived by the bulk of the Middle Eastern populace as controlled by Washington and popular forces for change, including the grass-roots Islamist movements supported by Iran.

In terms of the implications of the overthrow of Saddam for the immediate regional political relations, as Ray Takeh has argued, the "rise of the Shi'ite community in Iraq is likely to portend better relations with Iran, as many of Iraq's leading Shi'ite political actors have close and intimate ties with the Islamic Republic" (Takeh 2008, p. 1). There is little doubt that the emergence of an Iraqi government dominated by Shi'a politicians has led to closer and more amenable ties between Iraq and the Iranian government. At the very least, Iran has profited strategically from the rise of a Shi'a-controlled Iraq whose principal leaders are drawn from Shi'a Islamist movements, the Supreme Council for the Islamic Revolution in Iraq (SCIRI) and the Dawa Party. The more sanguine relations between Baghdad and Tehran overturn almost four decades of animosity between the two neighbours. While in itself this portends to a more favourable situation in the region, the reaction of Arab states to this state of affairs has led to a dangerous regional Cold War.

Tehran's interests in the region seem to have elicited an overreaction from Middle Eastern leaders and the former US administration. Claims that Iraq's new government is a proxy of Iran, or that Hezbollah and Hamas are controlled from Tehran, serve to undermine the local grievances that are responsible for militancy. A more nuanced view of the

Middle Eastern and Iranian interests in Iraq is, in reality, very similar to those of the US and other states in the Middle East, in seeking to "prevent Iraq from once more emerging as a military and ideological threat" (Takeh 2008, p. 1). The Iranian government cannot risk further instability and violence in Iraq, nor is the Iranian leadership willing to oversee the dismemberment of its neighbour.[2] The US presence in Iraq is double-edged for Iran. On the one hand, Iran is aware that the US knows that the safety of American troops and the future of the American mission in Iraq relies on Shi'a endorsement, which has the potential to be influenced by the political interests from across the border in Tehran. On the other hand, there will be a continuing anxiety in Tehran for as long as there is a massive deployment of US troops in such close proximity to the Iranian border. There is still a danger that the US-Israel alliance will launch an attack on Iran in an effort to reduce the Iranian influence across the Middle East. While this scenario is unlikely, especially since the election of what seems to be a more diplomatic US administration under Barak Obama, the perception that Iran poses a danger to regional and international peace may ultimately prove to be a catalyst for further military intervention by the US and its Middle East allies.

More alarming than the Shi'a/Iranian resurgence is the way that the Iraq war has added to the radicalisation of the Middle Eastern attitudes to the outside world, only a little over a decade after the end of the Islamist-US alliance which vanquished the Soviet Union in Afghanistan. Many analysts have commented on the role of the (not so) covert US anti-Soviet strategy of supporting Islamist movements in the 1970s and 1980s (Cooley 2002; Lansford 2003; Dreyfus 2005). By the end of the ten-year war in Afghanistan, tens of thousands of Muslims, mainly from Arab states, had received extensive military training in the numerous camps along the Pakistani-Afghani border. The most widely known of the Islamic extremists to train in Pakistan and operate in Afghanistan are Osama bin-Laden and Ayman al-Zawarihi, today leaders of the terrorist network Al-Qaeda. Thousands of other Muslim extremists returned to their home countries victorious in their struggle against the Soviets with every intention to liberate their own societies from what they

---

2 Iran's Speaker of the Parliament made this an explicit point in 2005.

perceived to be extremely corrupted Muslim governments. In Egypt, Algeria, Saudi Arabia, Syria and Jordan, radical Islamic terrorists were responsible for thousands of civilian deaths. The veterans of the Afghan campaign declared a war on their fellow Muslims that would claim hundreds of thousands of lives in Algeria, and destabilise the region. The reach of Islamist extremists went beyond the immediate impact of the Middle East. As one analyst has argued in regards to the long-term impact of Afghanistan, "the legacy of that conflict, including well-trained terrorist operatives and a worldwide Islamist machine, would continue to plague the United States and the West" (Dreyfuss 2005, p. 302).

The Iraq war provided another opportunity for radical Islamists to enlist disaffected youth and angry Muslims into a liberationary struggle against a non-Muslim invader. Even before the fall of Baghdad, the call for a jihad against US forces was heard across the Muslim world from the prestigious Al-Azhar University to the communiqués from the concealed leadership of Al-Qaeda. What became clear in the days leading to the US invasion was that moderate and extremist Muslims alike viewed the planned invasion of Iraq as a strike against Islam (Shadid 2003). How many Muslims travelled to Iraq to join Abu Musab al-Zarqawi's Al Qaeda in the Land of the Two Rivers terrorist organisation is unclear. While the US inflated the numbers of foreign fighters in Iraq as a way of deflecting some of the attention from the size of the insurgency against US occupation, the number of Muslims that joined al-Zarqawi was in the thousands. According to Thomas Sanderson of the Washington-based Center for Strategic International Studies (CSIS), "Iraq has become a superheated, real-world academy for lessons about weapons, urban combat and terrorist trade craft" (Sanderson, cited in Rotella 2005). While the number of jihadists from Iraq was far less than the extraordinary number that trained and fought in Pakistan and Afghanistan in the 1980s, the risk of radicalised Islamic terrorists skilled in terrorism operations carrying on their struggle in their home countries is a major concern across the region. The "sad irony" of the US 'war on terror' in Iraq, Fawaz Gerges insists, is that it has "proved to be counterproductive to the struggle against the global jihad movement and has alienated the floating middle of Muslim public opinion. It has given Al Qaeda central and its affiliates a new lease on life" (Gerges 2006).

The increase in Islamic extremist activity in the Middle East as a consequence of the US invasion and occupation of Iraq remains a worrying security issue even if the violence in Iraq seems to have subsided. The Islamic extremism fuelled by events in Iraq since 2003 is representative of a much more worrying trend of escalating anti-American and anti-Western sentiments across the region.

How the US lost 'hearts and minds' in the Middle East

It is important to view the Arab attitude to the US as an accumulated set of grievances with Iraq and Afghanistan, and as clarifying a position many people in the Middle East had started to adopt prior to 2003. There is little doubt that the hard power of the US reached its zenith with the military occupation of Iraq in 2003. But American 'soft power' had declined substantially from the heights of the 1990s when under US auspices an era of peace was seemingly dawning on the Middle East. The US had overseen an end to the sectarian violence in Lebanon in 1989, US assistance had saved Afghanistan from the Soviet threat, and what seemed to be the crowning achievement of US diplomacy elicited widespread applause when on 13 September 1993 Yasser Arafat and Yitzhak Rabin shook hands on the lawn of the White House. The Israeli-Palestinian agreement, later to be known as the Oslo Accords, may not have led to acclaim from the Arab states of the Middle East but was seen as a step towards achieving justice for the Palestinian people. While predictions of an 'end of history' were being challenged by events in the Balkans and Rwanda, there seemed to be a real sense that the post-Cold War configuration was having a more positive impact on conflict in the Middle Eastern context. However, in the space of less than a decade the Middle East has become, to many commentators, the most violent and unstable region in the world and for the people of the Middle East, blame for the current state of affairs principally rests with the US.

In some ways the US attitude and behaviour towards the Middle East in the 1990s can be said to have brought about the destruction of the goodwill Middle Easterners felt towards American values and foreign policy. When Bernard Lewis (1990) asserted a 'clash of civilizations' between the US and the Muslim world, he was projecting onto all Muslims the attitudes of a very small minority of Muslims who were antagonistic to the spread of 'Western freedoms'. Samuel Huntington (1993), in the highly dubious work titled 'The clash of civilizations', made Lewis' polemic accessible to international relations and foreign policy intellectuals and practitioners. However, what both Lewis and Huntington obscured was that they were describing the views of the far-right of the Islamist movement rather than the Middle Eastern mainstream. By the time radical Muslim terrorists had caused massive death and destruction inside the US itself, many Middle Easterners were starting to question both US foreign policy and the sincerity of the US to the liberal-democratic model, but had not accepted the dichotomy of the 'clash of civilizations' as argued by Lewis and Huntington. Despite the best efforts of Osama bin Laden and the Islamist radicals on one side and the neo-conservatives on the other side to construct a 'clash of civilizations' in the post-September 11 era, the 'West' and 'Islam' have not entered into a direct confrontation. The terrorist attacks by Al Qaeda and the increasing antipathy to the US by Middle Easterners are unrelated.

Middle Eastern attitudes to the US had definitely soured as they witnessed Israeli contravention of the Oslo Accords and the unwillingness of the US to force successive Israeli governments to abide by the Oslo agreements.[3] In addition, the sanctions regime imposed on Iraq since 1994 by the Clinton government had been widely seen to have visited a major humanitarian disaster on Iraqi civilians, and in particular, on Iraqi children. The images of sick and starving Iraqi children that were regularly shown on Middle Eastern television and in Middle Eastern newspapers were convincing proof of the cruelty of American policy-makers and their wholesale disregard for Arab/Muslim lives. Despite opposition, even anger, from the Middle East to the sanctions and US policy towards the Israel-Palestine issue, a Pew survey in the days immediately after 9/11 found that as many people in the Middle East had a favourable attitude to the US as those that didn't (Pew Research Center for the People and the Press 2001). As these figures suggest, the events

---

3 In the first Arab Opinion Poll taken in 2002, the plight of the Palestinians ranked as the major issue for the respondents. Of course, a series of Palestinian terrorist attacks on Israeli citizens dramatically complicated matters as did the assassination of Yitzhak Rabin in 1996.

of 9/11 did not vindicate Lewis and Huntington as many immediately claimed. Rather, the clamour in the US to accept the saliency of the 'clash of civilizations' has resulted in a self-fulfilling prophecy. The Middle Eastern attitude has been shaped since 2001 by the conduct of the US in Iraq and Afghanistan. Middle Eastern public opinion recoils from the images and narratives they are presented with of the brutality of the US invasion of Iraq, the revelations of US interrogation techniques at Abu Ghraib and Guantánamo Bay and the sense of US complicity in the intensification of Israeli belligerence in the region.

The real turning point for the Middle East in terms of their relationship with the US was the invasion of Iraq and the belief from Iran to Morocco that the US invasion was a war against Iraqis, against Arabs, and against Muslims. According to a 2008 survey conducted by Shilbey Telhami, eighty-one per cent of the respondents drawn from Egypt, Saudi Arabia, Jordon, Morocco, the United Arab Emirates and from Lebanon believed that Iraqis were worse-off (with only two per cent believing Iraqis were better-off) after the US invasion than under Saddam Hussein (Telhami 2008). In the same survey, sixty-one per cent of the respondents had a very unfavourable attitude towards the US and sixty-five per cent did not believe that the US was interested in spreading democracy in the Middle East. The cynicism towards the US in the Middle East in 2008 had risen dramatically since 2002 when the first poll was taken, and according to James Zogby, a long-time observer of Arab public opinion and the director of the Washington based Arab-American Institute:

> Negative attitudes hardened ... And we found that the major reasons that they hardened had to do with Iraq. Iraq has replaced Israel-Palestine for the time being as the principal source of aggravation ... The [U.S. in Iraq] treatment of Arabs and Muslims is a strong second for most of the countries (cited in Tate 2005).

The results of the Arab Opinion Poll are backed up by the Pew Global Attitudes Project Surveys which also tracks attitudes to the US (Pew Research Center 2005; Kohut 2005). Turkey, a long-time ally of the US, scored the lowest among the forty-seven countries where the survey was conducted, with only nine out of one hundred Turks holding a favourable view of the United States, down a stunning forty-three percentage points from a US State Department survey in 2000. In the view of Andrew Kohut and Richard Wike writing for the US-based *National Interest* magazine, the decline in the positive attitudes held towards the US by Muslims was attributed to "[t]he war in Iraq" which they argued "both solidified anti-Americanism in the Arab Middle East and extended it to other parts of the Muslim world, such as Turkey and Indonesia" (Kohut & Wike 2008).

In most 'Western countries', the images and reports of the war in Iraq in 2003, as in Afghanistan in 2001, and previously in Iraq in1991, favoured the US government and military interpretation of the surgical techniques and low-cost in terms of civilian casualties in the method of warfare conducted by the US. Increasingly, it was revealed that US bombs which only fell on 'military targets', 'sparing civilians' was shown to be an illusion resulting from the US military control of the media (Fairness and Accuracy in Reporting 2003; Monbiot 2005; Moody 2005). The civilian casualties may not have figured highly on the US accounting of the war but across the Middle East reports of the Iraqi dead and wounded were widely circulated. Even moderate press agencies like Egypt's *Al-Ahram* ran stories on the atrocities committed by coalition forces against Iraqi civilians. As early as April 2003, only five weeks after the war had been launched, an article in *Al-Ahram* challenged the 'Western press' to report Iraqi civilian deaths more accurately, citing the numerous reports of civilian casualties from US missiles that were being completely ignored by the US press and media (Abdel-Latif 2003). Highlighting the difference between the stories seen on 'Western' news outlets with those in the Middle East, the article continues,

> Al-Jazeera, along with a barrage of Arab TV satellite stations, such as the one-month-old Al-Arabiyya, Abu Dhabi TV, the Beirut-based LBC/Al-Hayat and Future TV, have helped shape the perceptions of viewers across the Arab world on how the war is progressing … causing some observers to argue that if there has been an emphasis on US and UK channels on allied victories, patriotism and flag-waving, then on Arab channels there has been a corresponding emphasis on coalition losses and civilian deaths, each set of channels playing to their respective audiences.

The war in Iraq, as seen from the Middle East perspective, has resulted in death and destruction for the Iraqi people, so that "Arab viewers have already made a choice ... For them, this is an illegal war of aggression" (Abdel-Latif 2003). Little has changed in the Middle Eastern mood since 2003 when *Al-Ahram* ran that story, except that as the Telhami survey has shown, the attitude towards the US has hardened. The post-September 11 policies of George W. Bush and his administration were designed, or so he told the world, to win the hearts and minds of Muslims, but as events in Iraq unfolded, what became increasingly clear was that the potential for the US to foster goodwill in the Middle East was lost forever amongst the carnage of the US invasion and the devastation suffered by the Iraqi people during the US occupation. However, while the US military hold over the Middle East appears stronger than ever – having deployed over 100,000 troops in Iraq and created permanent military bases in Qatar and Bahrain, as well as the proxy power of the Israeli Defence Forces at the disposal of Washington – the US today is suffering from an image problem that will continue to undermine its position in the region for years to come. The fall of Saddam Hussein was supposed to have led to the transformation of the Middle East as one authoritarian government after another fell to the inexorable forces of democracy unleashed by the US overthrow of Saddam Hussein. Eight years after Saddam was ousted from power, there has been little discernible change in the architecture of Middle East political systems.

The Iraq war and the subsequent public relations disaster that has befallen the US in the Middle East have turned democratic transformation of the region into a risky business. There is now a perception amongst US policy-makers that if democratic transformation occurred in the Middle East, friendly governments would fall and the governments that would come to power will have one thing in common: a deep distrust of the US and an antipathy for US foreign policy and interests. Thus, one of the lasting results of the US invasion and occupation of Iraq has been to ensure that democracy in the Middle East now receives less support from the US than it would have prior to 2003. This is but one of the ironies of the US intervention in Iraq – one of the few ironies amongst the many tragedies resulting from the irresponsible and immoral decision by the Bush and Blair governments to invade Iraq in 2003.

Iraq and the unravelling of US hegemony in the Middle East

It is certainly premature to predict that US power in the Middle East is about to be eclipsed anytime in the immediate future. However, the US invasion of Iraq and the subsequent ongoing occupation of that country have drastically undermined US soft power in the region. In particular, Iran has benefited most from the erosion of the US position in the Middle East, even as US troops continue to sit on Iran's western border. Rather than a Shi'a crescent emerging after the overthrow of Saddam and the advance of Shi'a power in Iraq, a more likely scenario is the rise of an anti-American crescent constituted by both Sunni and Shi'a opposition to the US and its Middle Eastern allies. Already, the Shi'a Hezbollah is considered a positive force by many in the Middle East – Sunni and Shi'a alike – due to its continued opposition to Israel in Palestine, and the US in Iraq. The US presence in Iraq has led to a moderation in the Sunni-Shi'a divide, which while overstated in some quarters, has existed for centuries in one form or another. Iran's re-emergence as a significant player in Middle Eastern affairs also benefited from the revenues it accrued during a period of high oil prices, but these are now on the wane since the heady days of US$150 a barrel in 2008. A weak Iraq with a Shi'a-dominated government has provided Iran with security and with the opportunity to project its influence into the Gulf in a way that it could not have anticipated prior to the US invasion of Iraq. In the words of Philip Robins, Iran "had been a threefold beneficiary of the US war in its western neighbour" (2008, p. 298).

Overall, the US invasion of Iraq with its huge death toll and devastation, torture, and the sectarian violence that ensued has ensured that the US position in the Middle East is dramatically weaker than ever before (Telhami 2007, p. 107). US soft power already under challenge in the Middle East after reaching a post-Cold War apogee in the early 1990s was decisively and definitively impaired by the brutality and illegality of the invasion of Iraq. While some people may have attributed the events that occurred in 2003 to George W. Bush and his neo-conservative administration, many in the Middle East are less sanguine and consider the entire US system at fault. The entrenching of the anti-US sentiment in the Middle East is so deep that not even the Messiah-like figure of Barak Obama will be able to restore Middle Eastern confidence in the US without a major breakthrough in the Israeli-Palestinian conflict and the complete withdrawal of troops from Iraq. In the meantime, the legacy of the US invasion is deepest in Iraq but resonates in a number of negative ways across the entire Middle East and will do so for years to come.

References

Abdel-Latif, O. (2003). Shockingly awful. *Al-Ahram*, no. 632, 3–9 April. Retrieved from weekly.ahram.org.eg/2003/632/sc19.htm.

Al Jazeera (2005). A new chapter to open in Iran-Iraq relations. *Al Jazeera*, July 7.

Cole, J. (2006). A 'Shi'a Crescent'? The regional impact of the Iraq war. *Current History*, 105(687): 20–26.

Cooley, J.K. (1999). *Unholy wars: Afghanistan, America and international terrorism*. London: Pluto Press.

Dreyfuss, R. (2005). *Devil's game: how the United States helped unleash fundamentalist Islam*. New York: Metropolitan.

FAIR (2003). TV not concerned by cluster bombs. *Fairness and Accuracy in Reporting*, May 6.

Gerges, F. (2006). Iraq war fuels global Jihad. *YaleGlobal*, 21 December. Retrieved from yaleglobal.yale.edu/display.article?id=8577.

Haaretz Service (2009). Peres: clash between Iran, Sunni Arabs is inevitable. *Haaretz*, April 13. Retrieved from www.haaretz.com/hasen/spages/1078213.html.

Hanna, M.W. (2009). The reawakened specter of Iraqi civil war. *Middle East Report Online*, April.

Hourani, A.H. (1991). *A history of the Arab peoples*. Cambridge, Massachusetts: Harvard University Press.

Huntington, S.P. (1993). The clash of civilizations. *Foreign Affairs*, 72(3): 22–49.

International Crisis Group (2008). *Failed responsibility: Iraqi refugees in Syria, Jordan and Lebanon*, July. Retrieved from www.crisisgroup.org/home/index.cfm?id=5563.

Kohut, A. (2005). Testimony to United States House of Representatives International Relations Committee Subcommittee on Oversight and Investigations, November 10. Retrieved from www.au.af.mil/au/awc/awcgate/congress/koh111005.pdf.

Kohut, A. & Wike, R. (2008). All the world's a stage. *The National Interest*, June 5. Retrieved from www.nationalinterest.org/Article.aspx?id=17502.

Lansford, T. (2003). *A bitter harvest: US foreign policy and Afghanistan*. Aldershot, England: Ashgate.

Lewis, B. (1990). The roots of Muslim rage. *The Atlantic*, 266(3): 47–60.

Monbiot, G. (2005). The media are minimizing US and British war crimes in Iraq. *The Guardian*, November 8.

Moody, B. (2005). Reuters says US troops obstruct reporting of Iraq. *Reuters*, September 8.

MSNBC (2004). Hardball with Chris Matthews. December 9. Retrieved from www.msnbc.msn.com/id/6679774.

Pew Research Center (2005). Global opinion: the spread of anti-Americanism. *Trends 2005*, Pew Research Center, Washington, pp. 122–37.

Pew Research Center for the People and the Press (2001). America admired, yet its new vulnerability seen as good thing, say opinion leaders, December19. Retrieved from people-press.org/report/?pageid=60.

Robins, P. (2008). The war for regime change in Iraq. In L. Fawcett (Ed.). *International relations of the Middle East*, 2nd ed. Oxford: Oxford University Press.

Rotella, S. (2005). Bringing Jihad home to Europe. *Los Angeles Times*, September 23.

Shadid, A. (2003). Scholars urge Jihad in event of Iraq war. *Washington Post*, March 11.

Shilbey, T. (2007). America in Arab eyes. *Survival*, 49(1): 108.

Sirriyeh, H. (2007). Iraq and the region since the war of 2003. *Civil Wars*, 9(1): 106–25.

Takeh, R. (2008). Iran's new Iraq. *The Middle East Journal*, 62(1): 13–30.

Tate, D. (2005). Negative attitudes toward US remain in Arab world. *Voice of America*, December 7. Retrieved from www.voanews.com/english/archive/2005-12/2005-12-07-voa87.cfm?CFID=178505592&CFTOKEN=22858573&jsessionid=8830b9ece85ff54fcf09442f502c2c137c6a.

Telhami, S. (2008). 2008 annual Arab opinion poll. Retrieved from www.brookings.edu/topics/~/media/Files/events/2008/0414_middle_east/0414_middle_east_telhami.pdf.

PART TWO
Nonviolent alternatives

6
Between Iraq and a hard place
Michael Otterman

The images, taken in January 2008, depict Iraqi refugees in Sayda Zainab, a Damascus enclave that holds around 50,000 Iraqis. Every morning over a dozen buses in Sayda Zainab return Iraqis to the country they once called home. Other Iraqis beg for spare change while homeless children, prowling street cats, motorbikes, pushcarts, trucks, buses and old taxis vie for space on the crowded laneways.

Fig 1. Prayer beads for sale in one of the busy stalls in Sayda Zainab.

Fig 2. Iraqi family walks through the streets of Sayda Zainab.

Fig 3. Young boy pauses while playing with friends in an empty lot in Sayda Zainab.

Fig 4. Woman in front of the Shrine of Sayda Zainab – believed to contain the remains of the Prophet Mohammed's granddaughter.

Fig 5. Young boy shouts 'goodbye' to a bus departing to Baghdad from the Sayda Zainab bus depot.

Fig 6. An Iraqi Kurd in Sayda Zainab displays the photograph of his kidnapped son.

Fig 7. An Iraqi family sees off family members returning to Baghdad from Sayda Zainab.

Fig 8. Bus driver collects passports before departure to Baghdad. A one-way ticket from Sayda Zainab costs roughly AU$10.

Fig 9. Owner and driver of the Gold Eagle stands proudly in front of his bus prior to departure to Baghdad.

7
Coalition of the unwilling: the phenomenology and political economy of US militarism
Jake Lynch

America taught us to be modern, then postmodern. New York, said the English novelist Martin Amis, who settled there, is where they "road-test the future". Hollywood provided the pictures, and rock'n'roll the soundtracks, for the popular imagination of successive generations.

At the same time, the insistent backbeat of conflict has been supplied by Americans too, in a percussive hail of bombs, bullets and shells. The US entry into World War II culminated in the nuclear attacks on Hiroshima and Nagasaki, a technological triumph which simultaneously called into question the philosophical underpinnings of modernity. History might be moving, not in forward progress to enlightenment but backwards towards apocalypse, a sense captured in the enigmatic opening of *Gravity's rainbow*, the 1973 novel by Thomas Pynchon. Some of the action is set in wartime London, cowering under the threat of the German V-2 rocket, forerunner of today's ballistic missiles. Seeming to refer, simultaneously, to nuclear annihilation, the book begins: "A screaming comes across the sky. It has happened before, but there is nothing to compare it to now. It is too late" (Pynchon 1973, p. 3).

This fear – that we might all suddenly be reduced to nothingness on little more than the whim of a middle-ranking military officer – was explored a decade earlier in the Stanley Kubrick movie, *Doctor Strangelove*. At the time, the same dread brought thousands out on to the streets in anti-nuclear protests, perhaps most notably around Britain's Atomic Weapons Research Establishment at Aldermaston in southern England.

For all that, majorities in the US, UK and allied countries spent the Cold War decades learning, as the subtitle of Kubrick's film has it, "to stop worrying and love the bomb". When the Campaign for Nuclear Disarmament was revived in the 1980s, Michael Heseltine, then Britain's Defence Secretary – a charismatic speaker, whose persuasive powers were in no way diminished by a slight speech impediment – famously labelled us an "unwepwesentative minowity".

The 'Atlanticist' argument was sustained by several important myths. Nuclear weapons kept the peace, one argument proposed, because the balance of missiles on either side of the Iron Curtain imposed restraint through the certainty of MAD, 'mutually assured destruction', if ever one was actually fired off. Actually, the North Atlantic Treaty Organisation had a policy called 'flexible response', a euphemism concealing plans for a first nuclear strike, if that was required to repel Moscow's tank battalions rolling into Western Europe.

But the most persuasive line, which I remember ruefully from unsuccessful attempts to convince my peers in school debates, pub conversations and political meetings, was simple: "if they've got them, we must have them". It was, in other words, the formation of the conflict as a gigantic tug-of-war, which exerted the strongest disciplinary effect on political discourses about military affairs in general, and nuclear weapons in particular. Around this was built a vast 'security' apparatus comprising both these elements – political and military – and also, of course, commercial interests.

America's participation in the struggle against Hitler (and in the Pacific theatre, the Japanese) had shifted the course of events decisively in favour of the eventual victors – not, as commonly supposed in the West, 'the allies', depicted in countless war movies as uniformly Anglophone, but the United Nations. President Truman greeted news of the end of the war in Europe with the words: "General Eisenhower informs me that the forces of Germany have surrendered to the United Nations" (Truman 1945). The document that formalised the Nazi defeat includes these words: "This Act of Military Surrender is without prejudice to, and will be superseded by, any general instrument of surrender imposed by, or on behalf of, the United Nations on Germany" (Act of Military Surrender, 1945).

This came several years after twenty-six countries, including China and the Soviet Union, signed up to the Atlantic Charter, forerunner of the UN Charter. The signing of that document, in 1945, was the culmination of a complex military and political effort that began after Pearl Harbour four years earlier. "Understanding the UN's wartime origins provides a powerful and much-needed reminder that the world body is not some liberal accessory but was created out of hard, political necessity as a strategic engine of victory" (Plesch 2005).

The military-industrial complex

General Eisenhower succeeded Truman in the White House and led America into battle in Korea, but perhaps his most significant political gesture came as he left the Oval Office. Eisenhower used his farewell speech to warn Americans and the world that the historic achievement of defeating fascism was in danger of being subverted by the "military-industrial complex" (Eisenhower 1961).

The UN Charter effectively made aggressive war illegal. It was the centrepiece of a decisive shift in global governance, based on a normative assumption that from then on countries would only resort to military force if they themselves were attacked. This was the fruit of victory, planted by political necessity and cultivated by negotiation and compromise. And Eisenhower's point? That doesn't suit everyone. The UN was intended to put to bed the principle of 'might is right'. But the mighty – in this case, the vested interests in the war industry – now threatened to attain what he called a "disastrous rise of misplaced power" over the way we decide to respond to conflicts and crises, and they did so by framing them in terms of right and wrong.

The bipolar formation of the Cold War lent itself to this project. In October 1945, Truman had produced twelve points to govern American policy, including the importance of opening up free markets (Alexander 2002). The program would be based on "righteousness", he said: there would be "no compromise with evil". As after previous wars, the president had commissioned a review of US forces, but, uniquely in American history, this resulted in a decision not to winnow them back down to previous levels (Hossein-Zadeh 2006), but rather to maintain them at something like the degree of readiness required to engage in two major theatres of war – such as Europe and the Far East – at the same time. It's no accident that this has been the core Pentagon doctrine ever since. The political will was generated through the most extraordinary official campaign of demonisation and propaganda, the 'red scare' of McCarthyism, which led to the paradigm of identity and alterity – self and other, or 'us' and 'them' – becoming institutionalised at all levels of US society.

The next imposture came with war in Vietnam, presented as a necessary measure to prevent the countries of south-east Asia falling like 'dominoes' into the clutches of communism. America's defeat, a decade later, came during the era of *détente*, when arms control agreements with the Soviet Union were easing tensions between the superpowers – tensions that had kept the upward pressure on military preparations and budgets. The Non-Proliferation Treaty, limiting access to the bomb and committing nuclear-armed states to enter into substantive negotiations to reduce and eliminate their arsenals, came into force in 1970, quickly followed by the Strategic Arms Limitation Treaty of 1972.

Between them, these developments posed a threat to the interests of the military-industrial complex and triggered a notable new exertion of what Eisenhower had called its "unwarranted influence ... in every city, every State house, every office of the Federal government" (Eisenhower 1961). In Washington, CIA appraisals of the receding threat from Moscow were brushed aside by a team convened on the orders of President Gerald Ford – keen to prove, perhaps, that he really could walk and chew gum at the same time – to pore over the same field reports and raw data, and second-guess the assessments drawn up by the agency's top analysts.

Team B, as it was known, reached some startling conclusions. No evidence could be found to support the long-held fear that the Soviets had developed an acoustic system for detecting US nuclear submarines ... so they must have developed an undetectable, non-acoustic one instead. Moscow's air defences were in tip-top condition, the team decided, based on the unimpeachable evidence of boasts in an official Russian training manual. A book on Soviet military strategy titled *The art of winning* was translated as *The art of conquest* (Curtis 2004).

This period can be viewed in retrospect as a crisis of military legitimacy, the first of three notable examples in recent times. A prime mover in the agitation for Team B was Donald Rumsfeld, Ford's Secretary of Defense, later to resume, of course, under George W. Bush. And the study's conclusions were taken up by a well-resourced ginger group calling itself the Committee on the Present Danger, which then projected its warnings via media messages to the general public and lobbying approaches to politicians, including presidential hopeful Ronald Reagan.

Reagan's election victory of 1980 ensured that, as in the late 1940s, the end of a war would not bring a reduction in military budgets but instead signal their relentless expansion. This project now met with well-organised opposition, however, both at home and abroad. My own CND activism came against the backdrop provided by the women's peace camp at Greenham Common, supposedly a base of Britain's Royal Air Force but significant as a launchpad for cruise missiles, part of the US nuclear arsenal. The appointment of Michael Heseltine, the most effective debater in Margaret Thatcher's Cabinet, to take us on, was a backhanded compliment.

And across the Atlantic, the 'Great Communicator' himself performed an abrupt about-turn, well before the arrival of Mikhail Gorbachev as a negotiating partner in Moscow, in response to the powerful Nuclear Freeze Movement. In a few short months, it fielded the biggest ever demonstration in New York's Central Park, and won 36 out of 39 referendums in eight states. Media and politicians alike were unable to ignore it, and Reagan was forced to disavow his administration's and NATO's own policy and declare a nuclear war "unwinnable". A ban on space weapons, proposals for a 'zero option' on nukes in Europe, and the Strategic Arms Reduction Treaty, all followed, including a rare cut in the Pentagon's budget.

It's important to emphasise that at the time the Soviet Union collapsed, US war preparations were actually being drawn down rather than stepped up, because it sets the scene, at the end of the Cold War, for another crisis of military legitimacy. Communism was seen to have imploded under the weight of its own contradictions, as conventional CIA analysis in the 1970s said it would. The diplomacy of Reagan and Gorbachev had helped to ensure its end was less painful than it could have been. Now, amid heady talk of Europe being healed of its wounds, millions looked forward to rebuilding better, more prosperous societies with the help of a so-called peace dividend – resources diverted from the military, which, of course, no longer needed them.

Elsewhere, the period after Vietnam saw the fall of governments friendly to Washington as far apart as Laos and Mozambique (both 1975), Nicaragua and Iran (both 1979) and even the Philippines (1986). Cambodia not only fell to the Khmer Rouge in 1975, it then took the Vietnamese themselves, in an invasion four years later, to remove the genocidal Pol Pot regime from power. The Reagan Doctrine saw efforts to stem the 'red tide' entrusted to proxy armies, such as the Contras in Nicaragua, and RENAMO and UNITA in southern Africa, since the deployment of America's own troops across other countries' borders had become a political lemon.

Towards Desert Storm

However, low-intensity warfare, in what were – to the American public and those of most allied countries – obscure, faraway places, did not meet the needs of the military-industrial complex. Ismael Hossein-Zadeh puts it well:

> Actual shooting wars are needed not only for the expansion but for the survival of this empire. Arms industries need occasional wars not only to draw down their stockpiles of armaments, and make room for more production, but also to display the 'wonders' of what they produce: the 'shock and awe'-inducing properties of their products and the 'laser-guided, surgical operations' of their smart weapons (2006, p. 19).

Through this same period, US involvement in shooting wars crept back on to the agenda, with the invasion of Grenada (1983), an aerial attack on Libya (1986) and the invasion of Panama (1989) representing limited, small-scale demonstrations of military capability. Then came the strategic switch to a new enemy, action against whom would bring arresting images of 'smart bomb' technology into millions of living rooms around the world.

The engagements of the 1980s had already presaged a transition from pursuing Cold War enmities to the prosecution of 'rogue' individuals and states. Colonel Gadaffi, whom Reagan dubbed 'Mad Dog', was targeted over his support for 'terrorism'. Manuel Noriega ('Pineapple Face') was wanted on drugs charges when his security forces shot and killed a US Marine, providing a pretext for eliminating him. The pretext was altogether stronger in the case of the next enemy to find himself in the cross-hairs: Iraqi president Saddam Hussein.

The escapade that put the Pentagon back in business, as the 'enforcement arm' of the 'international community', was Operation Desert Storm in 1991, in which an American-led multi-national force ejected Saddam's occupying troops from Kuwait. Suspicions over the role the US played behind the scenes centred on a meeting, the previous year, between Saddam himself and Washington's Ambassador in Baghdad, April Glaspie.

One version of the transcript has Glaspie saying:

> I have received an instruction to ask you, in the spirit of friendship – not confrontation – regarding your intentions: Why are your troops massed so very close to Kuwait's borders? ... We have no opinion on your Arab-Arab conflicts, such as your dispute with Kuwait. Secretary [of State, James] Baker has directed me to emphasize the instruction, first given to Iraq in the 1960s, that the Kuwait issue is not associated with America (*New York Times*, 23 September 1990).

It led to allegations that Glaspie had effectively given a green light to Iraq's invasion of its neighbour, a turn of events that took most of the world by surprise.

Stormin' Norman Schwarzkopf, the US army general who was to become a familiar figure in the months that followed, recalls a visit to Camp David to attend a cabinet meeting shortly after Saddam's *démarche*. The episode appears in his autobiography, *It doesn't take a hero* (1992). On the sidelines, he expressed scepticism to his boss, Colin Powell – then chairman of the Joint Chiefs of Staff – over the merits of US military action by way of response. Powell told Schwarzkopf: "I think we could go to war if they invaded Saudi Arabia. I doubt if we would go to war over Kuwait."

As if by magic, news then surfaced at the Pentagon that thousands of Iraqi troops were "massing" again, this time on the Saudi border, ready to pounce. President Bush began talking about Saddam Hussein as "the Hitler of the Middle East", bent on conquest and regional domination. The story was refuted by a reporter from a small Florida newspaper, the *St Petersburg Times*, who commissioned her own satellite pictures of the area from *Soyuz Karta*, a newly privatised arm of the former Soviet state, now touting for business from all comers. These pictures showed acres of empty desert – nothing more.

Was Desert Storm, then, a giant conspiracy? Did the US military-industrial complex somehow 'lure' Saddam Hussein, as a spider lures a fly, into a web from which there was no way out? Was there a plot, involving the diplomatic service, the White House and the military, to create a pretext for another major war, in order to show off the latest 'smart' weaponry being produced by the big Pentagon contractors and generate more orders?

To ask the question in those terms is to supply the answer, of course. To imagine active collusion taking place on the far-ranging scale required to bring about this sequence of events, and remaining hidden, would be far-fetched. However, there are indications of an in-built systemic momentum towards war – indications we can infer both from evidence of the organisational memory applied to media strategies, and an appreciation of the changing characteristics of the wider business environment in the US and elsewhere.

The phenomenology of America's wars

First, though, a diversion into phenomenology. Hossein-Zadeh presents "shooting wars" as "occasional", remember, a deviation from the norm; and that is, indeed, a prevalent view. For the US, however, it is now arguably the other way round. Consider: the American entry into World

War II came after the attack on Pearl Harbour, in December 1941, and lasted three and a half years. Then the Korean War lasted three years, and US military involvement in Vietnam, another nine years.

A series of brief encounters were followed by the anti-climactic rendezvous with Saddam Hussein's conscript army in the sands of Kuwait. That was in 1991, but it is worth asking, when did that war cease, and the next one begin? UN Security Council Resolution 687, which marked the end of Operation Desert Storm, also called on member states to do whatever they could to protect the Kurds in the north and the Shi'as in the south from Saddam's vengeance. The US, Britain and (initially) France interpreted this as a mandate to establish "no-fly zones" over the north and south of the country and began flying regular patrols.

Over the years, this developed into a game of cat and mouse, with claims that Iraq was coming closer to shooting down one of the planes involved, risking the attendant propaganda boost that would bring to the regime. So, military installations began to be targeted in the rest of the country as well. In December 1998, the Clinton administration ordered "Operation Desert Fox", a four-day series of strikes on alleged weapons research and development installations, air defence systems, weapon and supply depots, and the barracks and command headquarters of the Republican Guard.

At the same time, the US and its allies were pressing for ever more stringent sanctions, originally imposed by the UN as a way of preventing Iraq from developing so-called weapons of mass destruction, but intended by the US to continue, as President Bill Clinton once said, "until the end of time, or as long as he [Saddam Hussein] is still there" (Crossette 1997). Moreover, the list of banned goods included spare parts needed to repair sanitation systems damaged in 1991, without which Iraq's previous supply of clean drinking water became contaminated, leading to outbreaks of infectious diseases such as typhoid and cholera (as pointed out by Sue Wareham earlier in this book). The so-called oil-for-food program was supposed to provide for the basic humanitarian needs of Iraqi people, but, as the UN's former in-country coordinator, Hans von Sponeck, pointed out, the allotted sum of money amounted to just US$110 per person per year (2001).

In August 1999, the UN Sub-Commission on the Promotion and Protection of Human Rights requested the international law expert, Marc Bossuyt, prepare a working paper on 'The adverse consequences of economic sanctions on the enjoyment of human rights', which he then presented to the Sub-Commission's meeting in Geneva in August 2000. Bossuyt highlighted the serious violations of international human rights instruments applicable to the children of Iraq, declaring the sanctions regime to be tantamount to genocide. It was, he declared:

> Illegal under existing international humanitarian law and human rights law ... The sanctions regime against Iraq has as its clear purpose the deliberate infliction on the Iraqi people of conditions of life (lack of adequate food, medicine, etc.) calculated to bring about its physical destruction in whole or in part. It does not matter that this deliberate physical destruction has as its ostensible objective the security of the region (Bossuyt 2000).

Back in 1996, CBS *60 Minutes* reporter Lesley Stahl had tackled then Secretary of State Madeleine Albright, on air, on the unfolding horrors of the sanctions regime: "We have heard that a half million children have died. I mean, that's more children than died in Hiroshima. And, you know, is the price worth it?"

Albright's reply, "I think this is a very hard choice, but the price – we think the price is worth it" seemed to indicate an awareness of the cost the policy was exacting in terms of human lives – an implication notably ignored by most US media, both at the time and afterwards when Iraq kept resurfacing on the news agenda.

The point is, hostilities never actually stopped after Desert Storm. Iraq continued to be regarded as a legitimate theatre of US military operations, so that the invasion of 2003 represented the next, decisive intensification of an ongoing campaign, which had been waged meanwhile through military, diplomatic and economic means. In the process, the United Nations, indispensable to previous American triumphs in the world wars and the Gulf war, was eventually brushed aside. Given that President Barack Obama, upon taking office, set a timeline for "the end of our combat mission in Iraq" by August 2010, that puts the duration of the war on Iraq at 19 years, to add to the cumulative 16 and half years of the earlier engagements.

That means the time the US will have spent at war comes to 35 and a half out of the 69 years between 1941 and 2010 – more than half. It begs the question of how to count the coterminous war in Afghanistan. Perhaps the years since the country was invaded and occupied, in 2001, should count as double. Even without such a device, the phenomenology implied in Hossein-Zadeh's formula is now reversed, and likely to continue in the same direction.

The fact that, some time in the present decade, the US switched to a country whose *normal* state is to be at war is significant because it should lead us to view these wars, not as a series of one-off responses to individual 'threats' and 'crises', but as the product of a system. In phenomenological terms, it directs our attention to continuities, rather than particularities; and continuities, moreover, that show evidence of intensification over the period in question.

Media management

One continuity that has been traced and mapped is the evolution of message projection and management around the US use of force. Ottosen and Luostarinen interpret the rhetoric of Desert Storm, typified by the extravagant comparisons of Saddam Hussein with Hitler, as part of a deliberate marketing strategy to overcome the political problems of the Vietnam war, which

> grew on to the country's domestic political divisions and conflicts. Vietnam became transformed into a symbol that divided the political right and left and partly also different generations. One of the central tasks of Coalition information activities during the Gulf War was to prevent the domestic or international 'politicisation' of the war, to prevent it from being transformed into an event that could symbolize wider political divisions (2000, p. 43).

Moreover, they identify a series of techniques, also honed and refined in a continuous arc of endeavour since the days of Vietnam, for micromanaging the media. The invasion of Grenada, in 1983, drew complaints that reporters and camera crews had been kept away from all the significant action, and were therefore unable to bring their readers and audiences vivid field reports of the decisive battles. This neutralised the media threat, from the Pentagon perspective, but nullified any opportunity they might present. By 1991, therefore, a more positive approach had been developed: not only "punish journalists who engage in critical reporting; withhold information that can place own soldiers in a bad light" but also "use the media to misinform about the warfare" (Ottosen & Luostarinen 2000, pp. 45–46).

The application of these measures helped to ensure that definitional and representational power remained largely in the hands of military planners and their political masters, at least in this episode. In the next, however, the bombing of Yugoslavia in 1999, the Pentagon approach was outflanked, with the authorities in Belgrade organising quick-response "rubble tours" highlighting NATO bombing "errors" and the civilian casualties they left in their wake.

Philip Knightley, the veteran investigative reporter who wrote the classic history of war reporting, *The first casualty*, interprets the innovation of 'embedding' journalists and crews with forward units, in 'Operation Iraqi Freedom' in 2003, as the next response – a way to supply pictures of sufficiently dramatic intensity to win the competition for the top slot in global news bulletins, eclipsing reports illustrating the human cost (in Lynch 2008, p. 216). And, Knightley adds, the harassment and punishment of journalists operating outside the "pool" were stepped up.

As if to emphasise this last point, the critical Arab-owned TV station, *Al-Jazeera*, which brought its audiences many images of death and destruction caused by the "shock and awe" of the invasion, came under US fire at its offices in Kabul, Basra and Baghdad. The International Federation of Journalists stated: "it is impossible not to detect a sinister pattern of targeting" (White 2003).

The political economy of US militarism

As well as the observable, motivated process of intensification in the waging of warfare in the symbolic realm, the other key continuity-providing evidence that the US is now systematically predisposed to continuing engagement in significant-scale social violence is located in the economic sphere. During World War II, Charles E Wilson – later to become Eisenhower's Defense Secretary – told a hearing of the Army Ordnance Board that, to prevent another Great Depression, the United States needed "a permanent war economy".

The nature and structure of US capitalism have been transformed since the days of Wilson and Eisenhower, notably by the so-called "shareholder value revolution". Will Hutton, the UK economics writer who is now Chief Executive of the Work Foundation, chronicles the fortunes of General Electric, which delivered 80 consecutive quarters of profit growth under its legendary Chairman and CEO, Jack Welch. Welch presided over a tenfold increase in GE's market value, but transformed it, in the process, "into a half manufacturing, half financial services company" (2002, p. 26). Workers were incentivised by the prospect of dismissal, as the Reagan administration and its successors stripped away workplace protections. At the same time, spending on research and development, once the symbol of the firm's vitality and innovative capacity, fell below the US corporate average and continued to decline.

A famous speech by Welch himself, 'Growing fast in a slow-growth economy', delivered in New York in 1981, proved a landmark contribution to the debate over 'shareholder value'. The heavy gearing of Welch's own 'compensation' towards stock options typified the new 'alignment', Hutton records, between the interests of managements and shareholders. Moreover, such interventions transformed not merely the business climate, but also the political climate. Neo-liberalism, the set of economic policies adopted by governments with the avowed aim of freeing business to 'create wealth', successfully 'rolled back' social democracy, in the rich world, during the 1980s, and was then 'rolled out', via the International Financial Institutions, to the rest of the world, in the 1990s and beyond.

In many countries, governments were convinced or coerced to privatise state enterprises, monetise public goods and deregulate markets, in what amounted to a gigantic piggybank raid on the assets built up by previous generations. This one-off, 'ratcheting' effect matches the intensification manifest in the latter part of America's warfighting record since Pearl Harbour. Private contractors were the second biggest contingent of coalition forces in Iraq, after the US but ahead of the UK.

This historic switch having been accomplished, what Hutton describes as 'footloose capital' was left to seek ever more green fields from which to generate the stratospheric returns that stock markets had been led, by the likes of Jack Welch, to expect. Naomi Klein (2007) posits another phenomenological shift, parallel with the first, as a direct result of these conditions. It is generally assumed that business craves, above all else, 'stability' – a predictable context, subject only to gradual, incremental change – in which to operate. Now, however, it was only a 'clean sheet' or 'fresh start' that would open up sufficiently lucrative opportunities to enable market expectations to be met.

Klein (2007) examines the rapid economic transformations triggered by recent natural disasters. Hurricane Katrina permitted the wholesale privatisation of the New Orleans school system, where previously political opposition had ruled this out. The Asian tsunami devastated fishing communities along the Sri Lankan coast and thereby enabled long stretches of it to be parcelled up and apportioned to business interests in the name of 'reconstruction'.

It's a short step from the observation that business seeks out crises from which to profit – 'disaster capitalism', Klein calls it – to the next, namely that it thereby gains an interest in seeking to precipitate or even foment ever more extreme situations and events. Detailed plans for the economic transformation of Iraq were drawn up long before the invasion itself, she recounts, with policy prescriptions including "mass privatisation, complete free trade, a 15 percent flat tax, a dramatically downsized government" (Klein 2007, p. 8). The privatisation of warfighting functions, development aid and postwar reconstruction immerse government policy responses in the logic of what Frank Stilwell calls "profit-fuelled conflicts and interventions", where business adds to the "confluence of capital and opportunity" that creates conditions for social violence (2008, p. 263). The opening salvoes of Operation Iraqi Freedom represented payback on all the investment business had already made in preparing for both war and its aftermath.

So large and multifarious was the house that Jack built that General Electric came to encompass and illustrate – within its own range of activities – many of these connections. One of Welch's acquisitions was the television network, NBC, thereby putting GE in a position directly to influence public opinion in favour of war. It was, of course, already a major 'defense' contractor, poised to profit from military spending. Among the significant factors joining these dots are the growth of corporate PR and the proliferation of on-air pundits from corporate-funded think-tanks, espousing both business-friendly policies and – as in the case of the American Enterprise Institute, prime advocate of the "troop surge" – escalations of military activities.

In his award-winning film, *WMD: weapons of mass deception*, Danny Schechter makes the intriguing observation that the media industry was, at the time, looking to the Federal Communications Commission to further deregulate the industry in "rule changes that would benefit their bottom lines. There was a question raised: Did the FCC agree to waive the rules if the media companies agreed to wave the flag?"

Jeff Chester, Director of the Center for Digital Democracy, tells Schechter: "You don't go in and report critically on an administration that you hope will give you billions and billions of dollars in new policies"; especially as the FCC was chaired at the time by Michael Powell, son of Secretary of State Colin Powell. Ottosen and Luostarinen, moreover, point out that the transition at the Pentagon – from the Vietnam legacy of seeing media as part of the problem, to Desert Storm and the plan to exploit their potential as part of the solution in managing the public presentation of military operations – coincided with the tightening grip of ever larger corporate interests: "Structural changes in the media industry since the early 1980s have been characterized by increased control in the hands of some 50 transnational corporations" (2000, p. 14). This represents another significant intensification over the period under discussion.

A change?

Fallout from the Global Financial Crisis, together with the election of Barack Obama to the White House, piqued many appetites for change, both in the US and around the world. After all, even Jack Welch had by now recanted his earlier doctrine, telling an interviewer from the *Financial Times*: "On the face of it, shareholder value is the dumbest idea in the world … Shareholder value is a result, not a strategy … Your main constituencies are your employees, your customers and your products" (Guerrera 2009).

As Obama confirmed the extension of America's war on Afghanistan to neighbouring Pakistan, however, and promised to match military commitment with lucrative reconstruction contracts, the auguries appeared mixed. By now, the doom-laden narratives of previous conflicts – the 'red menace', the 'rogue leader', and the 'terrorist threat' – lay in pieces, eroded by the tides of history or shattered by exposure to the light, as when propaganda over Iraq's so-called weapons of mass destruction rapidly and conspicuously unravelled. Hossein-Zadeh deduces the *a priori* existence of the military-industrial complex from the mismatch between security imperatives and the level of spending on preparations for combat, and the biggest bills were now coming in just as the case for war was at its least compelling.

George W. Bush explicitly likened his so-called war on terrorism to the generational challenge posed by the Cold War, but it never convinced to anything like the same extent. In December 2001, shortly after the 9/11 attacks, three respected institutions – the Pew Research Centre, Princeton Survey Research Associates and the *International Herald Tribune* newspaper – joined forces to conduct an interesting poll. They identified 275 people of influence in politics, media, business and culture, in a total of 24 countries, and asked them whether they believed their compatriots saw the attacks as something America had brought upon itself – a response, in other words, to its foreign, military and economic policies and their perceived effect on people's lives. This view – what the writer and Sydney Peace Prize Laureate, Arundhati Roy, calls the "context side" in the "fierce, unforgiving fault line that runs through the contemporary discourse on terrorism" – was shared by large majorities in the Middle East, narrower majorities elsewhere, and fifty-eight percent overall.

If we accept that acts of political violence are indissociable from context, that they can be explained, if not excused, by people's experience of identifiable factors in everyday life, then it makes sense to talk about responses other than war. Indeed, months later, in March 2002, leaders of 50 poor countries gathered in Monterrey, Mexico, to press for greater collective action to meet the Millennium Development Goals set by the UN to halve global poverty by 2015, and speakers lined up to link this project directly to the threat of 'terrorism'.

"In the wake of September 11, we will forcefully demand that development, peace and security are inseparable", declared UN General Assembly president Han Seung-soo. "To speak of development is to speak also of a strong and determined fight against terrorism", the conference heard, from then Peruvian president Alejandro Toledo. The quotes are taken from a report of the event by the Associated Press news agency, which opened with a line of context: "Leaders of poor nations warned their rich counterparts that if they want a world free of terrorism, they will need to pay for it" (Watson 2002).

Hard on the heels of the Monterrey meeting, figures released by the United Nations Conference on Trade and Development showed how poorer countries were being left behind as they opened their markets at the behest of International Financial Institutions. "We have seen a de-coupling of the trade engine from the growth engine in developing countries over the past two decades" was the verdict from UNCTAD Senior Economic Affairs Officer, Richard Kozul-Wright (Stewart 2002). The liberalisation of global trade, a central plank of neo-liberalism, was exacerbating inequality and injustice, the very issues most salient in the context Roy and others constructed for the 9/11 attacks and later incidents.

The poverty of Atlanticism

America is a classic example of a "polysemic" concept; any account of its history, politics or values must be a plural narrative. The sheer plenitude of US cultural production means we can each construct our 'own' distinctive version from a limitless supply of ideas and images, foreshadowed in Paul Simon's evocative lyric, 'We've all come to look for America'. Anatol Lieven (2004) divides the multiplicity of the US polity into two broad historical tributaries: on one hand, its "civic creed", beginning with the opening words of the Constitution, "We the People", and, on the other, a "Jacksonian" militarism.

Useful as Lieven's formulations are for conceptualising rival forms of nationalism, the present conjuncture has seen US responses to conflict, in effect, lifted out of either of these streams and launched, instead, into the unpredictable currents of corporate-driven globalisation. The author, William Pfaff, whose books appear on countless International Relations syllabi, used a syndicated column to recall the Great Transformation wrought upon capitalism by the industrial age, which "tore from their local roots the economic markets that since medieval times and before had been tied to communities, and had evolved through the needs and adaptations of those communities and their immediate neighbours" (Pfaff 2009).

This was, Pfaff (2009) pointed out, "the epoch that provoked socialism" and various efforts to "restore human values to economic life". Over the years this new version of capitalism had been "civilized, or half-tamed, until the arrival of globalization", whereupon "technology once again was eagerly used to destroy existing capitalism by repeating the two crimes of assassination that had destroyed the pre-capitalist economy: the use of technology to expand markets so widely as to destroy existing national and international regulations, and second, once again to commodify labor".

The gleaming artefacts of our postmodern, networked lifestyles – email, GPS, satellite TV – came out of America and stemmed, at least in part, from innovations by the military-industrial complex. That selfsame technology has extended the reach of markets, and amplified movements within them, to such an extent as to create conditions of intensifying toil, matched by corrosive uncertainty, even for the relatively well-off. What is so admired about the US is the flipside of what is mistrusted, resented and dreaded in much of the rest of the world. Even the appeal of the movies can no longer be entrusted purely to 'pull' factors. Naomi Klein (2007) observes that the destruction of the Iraqi state through "shock and awe" opened the country's borders, so that irreplaceable artefacts of its indigenous culture were looted from museums, packed up and shipped out, just as trucks thundered in with consignments of DVD players for sale in Baghdad's markets. A Pentagon planner, Major Ralph Peters, thus characterised the function of US armed forces in a post-Cold War world:

> There will be no peace. At any given moment for the rest of our lifetimes, there will be multiple conflicts in mutating forms around the globe. Violent conflict will dominate the headlines, but cultural and economic struggles will be steadier and ultimately more decisive. The de facto role of the US armed forces will be to keep the world safe for our economy and open to our cultural assault. To those ends, we will do a fair amount of killing (Peters 1997).

Events have rendered this logic visible to the extent that relationships with the US now bear the imprint of a third crisis of military legitimacy, following the earlier ones after Vietnam and the Cold War. Another survey, this time commissioned by the new United States Studies Centre, at the University of Sydney, revealed that in 2007, fully 48 percent of people in Australia – generally regarded as the most sedulous of all Washington's camp-followers – now favoured the adoption of an independent foreign policy at the expense of the US alliance.

Given the intensifying impetus to further wars, evidenced by the evolution of media strategies and underpinned by the corporate and political logic of neo-liberalism, the tensions uncovered by these polls, and manifest in global public discourses, are likely to carry on growing.

Any struggle for human values in economic and social life is in the opposite corner from the US military-industrial complex, and any effort to support or restore those values must now include, as a primary concern, opposition to America's wars. Contestation over news agendas – by Danny Schechter and many others – and attempts to roll back the hegemony of business lobbies over public policy-making, are part of the same fabric of resistance woven in earlier generations by the women of Greenham Common and the Nuclear Freeze Movement. It is now increasingly clear that calls for public intervention in global markets, to uphold workers' rights and protections, and support for continued military alliance with the United States – the time-honoured 'Atlanticist' position of mainstream opinion in trade union and labour movements in the rich world – are not compatible, but contradictory. The struggles can no longer be dissociated from one another.

References

Act of Military Surrender (1945). In *Official Gazette of the Control Council for Germany*. No. 1 Supplement, p. 6. Retrieved from www.ena.lu/act_military_surrender_berlin_1945-02-3797.

Alexander, A. (2002). The Soviet threat was a myth. *Guardian*, 19 April, London.

Bossuyt, M. (2000). The adverse consequences of economic sanctions on the enjoyment of human rights. *Global Policy Forum*. E/CN.4/Sub.2/2000/33. Retrieved from www.globalpolicy.org/component/content/article/202/42501.html.

Crossette, B. (1997). For Iraq: a doghouse with many rooms. *New York Times*, 23 November, New York, p. A4.

Curtis, A. (2004). *The power of nightmares*. BBC documentary.

Eisenhower, D.D. (1961). Eisenhower's Farewell Address to the Nation. Transcript, 17 January. Retrieved from www.h-net.org/~hst306/documents/indust.html.

Guerrera, F. (2009). Welch rues short-term profit 'obsession'. *The Financial Times*, 12 March. Retrieved from us.ft.com/ftgateway/superpage.ft?news_id=fto031220091430053057.

Hossein-Zadeh, I. (2006). *The political economy of US militarism*. London: Palgrave Macmillan.

Hutton, W. (2002). *The world we're in*. London: Little, Brown.

Klein, N. (2007). *The shock doctrine: the rise of disaster capitalism*. Melbourne: Allen Lane.

Lieven, A. (2004). *America right or wrong: an anatomy of American nationalism*. Oxford: Oxford University Press.

Lynch, J. (2002). *Reporting the world*. Taplow, UK: Conflict and Peace Forums.

Lynch, J. (2008). *Debates in peace journalism*. Sydney: Sydney University Press.

New York Times (1990). Excerpts From Iraqi Document on Meeting with U.S. Envoy. 23 September, Retrieved from www.chss.montclair.edu/english/furr/glaspie.html

Ottosen, R. & Luostarinen, H. (2000). The media Gulf War and its aftermath. In S.A. Nohrstedt & R. Ottosen (Eds). *Journalism and the new world order*. Gothenburg: Nordicom.

Peters, R. (1997). Constant conflict. *Parameters* (US Army War College Quarterly), Summer edition.

Pfaff, W. (2009). Welcome to suicidal capitalism. Weblog, 24 March. Retrieved from www.williampfaff.com/modules/news/article.php?storyid=387.

Plesch, D. (2005). The hidden history of the United Nations. Retrieved from www.opendemocracy.net.

Stewart, H. (2002). Poor miss out as rich nations cream off their trade. *The Guardian*, 30 April, UK. Retrieved from www.guardian.co.uk/business/2002/apr/30/globaleconomy.

Stilwell, F., Jordan, K. & Pearce, A. (2008). Crises, interventions and profits: a political economic perspective. *Global Change, Peace and Security*, 20(3): 263–74.

Tirman, J. (1999). How we ended the Cold War. *The Nation*, 1 November, New York.

Truman, S. (1945). Broadcast to the American People Announcing the Surrender of Germany. Transcript, 8 May, Washington DC. Retrieved from www.presidency.ucsb.edu/ws/index.php?pid=12241.

Von Sponeck, H. (2001). Sanctions on Iraq: a criminal policy that needs honest media coverage. *Media Development*, June edition, pp. 7–9.

Watson, J. (2002). Poor nations warn rich on terror. *Associated Press*, 22 March, Mexico. Retrieved from www.commondreams.org/headlines02/0322-05.htm.

White, A. 2003, International Federation of Journalists media release, 8 April.

8

Disarmament, demobilisation and rehabilitation: the pacifist dilemma

Isezaki Kenji

In light of the collusion in international armed conflict – such as involvement in Afghanistan (2001) and Iraq (2003) – the question of nonviolent alternatives remains. What international policy tool can underpin the nonviolent vision implicit in claims such as "Iraq, never again"? In deliberating our basic motives towards a common goal of global human security, it is my belief that the Responsibility to Protect (R2P) provides a great opportunity to both the military community and civil society. However, fundamental dilemmas need to be examined – such as the tensions between state sovereignty and human security; and, the paradox of 'peace'-keeping that requires the threat/use of military force. How are these tensions negotiated in order to realise the R2P opportunity? As the following anecdotes from my field placements in war zones suggest, the answer to this question lies in linking R2P and the notion of 'peace with justice'.

Introduction to R2P

The concept of R2P was born out of a Canadian initiative in 2001, deliberated at the United Nations World Summit of September 2005 and reaffirmed by UN Security Council Resolution 1674 in April 2006. I recently visited Ottawa to meet Lieutenant-General Roméo Dallaire, the former Force Commander of the United Nations Assistance Mission for Rwanda (UNAMIR). It was General Dallaire who introduced the concept of R2P to me. The discussions we had during my visit were filmed by the Japanese national broadcasting corporation NHK, who later broadcast a one-hour documentary and published a book of our discussions.[1]

R2P and General Dallaire are frequently spoken of with reference to Rwanda. In 1994, the genocide which took place in Rwanda killed over 800,000 people in just 100 days. General Dallaire was, at the time, Force Commander of the UN mission in Rwanda and he had detected signs of majority Hutus making deadly, all-out attacks on minority Tutsis. As an early preventative measure, he proposed to the UN Headquarters (UN HQ) Department of Peacekeeping Operations (DPKO) an intervention using military means, at least to seize caches of weapons that were being accumulated. His request was denied by headquarters. Subsequently, General Dallaire persistently proposed increasing the strength of his peacekeeping forces, including Rules of Engagement (ROE). These requests were consistently denied even after the genocide erupted and the international community became aware of the dire situation.

The UN HQ (with Kofi Annan heading up the DPKO) was afraid of losing its neutrality by using UN force against Hutus, even when faced with genocide. This UN attitude of non-interference was a result of what had happened the previous year in Somalia, where US soldiers who were part of the UN Peacekeeping Operation were killed and dragged through the streets by Somali militia. Footage of this scene was widely broadcast in the media and greatly affected US public sentiment regarding international peacekeeping missions. The Clinton administration, therefore, did not pressure the UN Security Council to intervene. As a result, General Dallaire was obliged to stand by and witness the terror of the Rawandan genocide. Today, as an elected senator in Canada, he is a strong advocate of R2P.

R2P essentially means that if a state ignores a gross violation of human rights, or becomes a part of it, the international community has the responsibility to intervene, even if this entails the use of military

---

[1] NHK Press (2007). *Recommendation for the future: Roméo Dallaire on building an era without the scourge of war* (in Japanese).

force. However, a tension between these two principles exists. That is, the principle of non-interference regarding state sovereignty, and the responsibility of the international community to respond to massive human rights violations, such as genocide and crimes against humanity. In my discussions with General Dallaire, this tension took on another dimension: the possibility that R2P could be used by sovereign states as an excuse for military aggression, as seen in the case of the 2003 occupation of Iraq sanctioned by the Bush administration. So, how do we implement R2P? How do we negotiate the principle of 'non-intervention' for legitimate cases and differentiate between a case that genuinely calls for R2P and a case that is being politically manoeuvred? The cue lies in linking peace with justice.

The case of Sierra Leone

Shortly after the September 11 attacks, a BBC World Service program focused on Africa. I listened to this broadcast while I was serving on the United Nations Mission in Sierra Leone (UNAMSIL) as Chief of Disarmament, Demobilisation and Reintegration (DDR). On this occasion a Sierra Leonean woman called from the nation's capital, Freetown. She said, "I would like to suggest to Mr George W. Bush the ultimate solution to end the war against the terror." The interviewer asked, "What is this?" and she replied, "this is to appoint Osama bin Laden as Vice-President of the United States." Another interviewer asked, "why do you think that is the ultimate solution?" She replied, "this is exactly what happened in Sierra Leone in order to stop the twelve-year war – appointing Foday Sankoh as the Vice-President of Sierra Leone. He was the person who had ordered the massacre of thousands of children." This appointment was brokered by the United States, and because of this, the final disarmament program for which I was responsible was about to start in Sierra Leone.

Foday Sankoh, the infamous head of the Revolutionary United Front (RUF), was the mastermind of the brutal twelve-year war in Sierra Leone. Another important figure was Charles Taylor, former president of Liberia who was the patron of RUF, an anti-government rebel group. Both Sankoh and Taylor made Sierra Leone infamous for 'blood diamonds'. Child solders were another sobering feature of the Sierra Leone war.

An estimated 300,000–500,000 people were killed and significant numbers cruelly tortured. So, how was this war ended? The final phase of the disarmament program started on 18 May 2001; disarmament and demobilisation were completed on 18 January 2002. We succeeded in disarming almost 50,000 combatants. President Kabbah then declared 'War Don Don'. This is a Creole expression meaning, 'War is over'. After four months of 'War Don Don', the first postwar general election was held and Kabbah was re-elected. However, there was also a much deeper story. In July of 1999, the controversial Lome Peace Accord was brokered. This was the key accord which led to the final disarmament program. In its article on 'Pardon and amnesty', the accord, "in order to bring lasting peace to Sierra Leone", granted Corporal Foday Sankoh absolute and free pardon, which was also extended to all combatants and collaborators. This extensive amnesty was an agreement not to pursue justice – even for war criminals.

As an annex of this accord, Foday Sankoh was given the post of Vice-President and also control of the Ministry of Natural Resources to control the 'blood diamonds'. Who brokered this accord? The US Clinton Administration appointed Reverend Jesse Jackson as Special Ambassador for Peace in Africa. Historically, the US has had a particular moral obligation to Liberia and its neighbour Sierra Leone since the emancipation of slaves. They tried to seek a solution that would not cost their own nation a single penny; that is, one that would not pursue justice in relation to war crimes. In doing so, they systematically ignored the pain of the victims and the global sense of justice. Due to this, anti-US sentiment rapidly grew among the people in Sierra Leone and this deal has now become something the US would rather forget.

At the time of the Lome Accord, the United Nations was silent. However, the UN took full advantage of the United States' action, securing the credit for ending the twelve-year war in Sierra Leone through its mission: Disarmament, Demobilisation and Reintegration. I have to admit, via the DDR program, we might have sent a terrible message to the next generation of Sierra Leoneans: that killing a few people is regarded as homicide, but in cases like this, the killing of thousands could be pardoned and even rewarded. A question we must ask ourselves is, how can R2P be a link to peace with justice?

The case of Japan

The concept of R2P and its links to peace with justice seem to be well understood by the Japanese public. This is because R2P is a built-in concept in the preamble of the Japanese Constitution, which has been unchanged since the end of World War II. It states:

> We, the Japanese people, desire peace for all time and are deeply conscious of the high ideals controlling human relationships, and we have determined to preserve our security and existence, trusting in the justice and faith of the peace-loving peoples of the world. We desire to occupy an honoured place in an international society striving for the preservation of peace, and the banishment of tyranny and slavery, oppression and intolerance for all time from the earth. We recognize that all peoples of the world have the right to live in peace, free from fear and want. We believe that no nation is responsible to itself alone, but that laws of political morality are universal; and that obedience to such laws is incumbent upon all nations who would sustain their own sovereignty and justify their sovereign relationship with other nations.
>
> We, the Japanese people, pledge our national honour to accomplish these high ideals and purposes with all our resources. (The Constitution of Japan, 3 November 1946)

However, there is a need to be vigilant in reaffirming the language and practice of peace with justice. As discussed above, politicians can use R2P as an excuse for military aggression. Indeed, the current and previous Japanese regimes have been riding this trend by sending our Self-Defense Force (SDF) abroad under claims about national interests. Even when the 'justice' of the war in Iraq is being seriously challenged – as demonstrated by the Republican election defeat in the US – Japanese statesmen are promoting support for an armed SDF to join US military engagements as a matter of strategic national interest. As a patriot, I feel ashamed that the Japanese public seems to support this argument. It is indeed a huge tragedy that R2P, a significant (although controversial) concept, will lose its noble foundation in Japan, for the sake of domestic politics; including significant governmental moves to abolish Article 9 of the Japanese Constitution – the clause renouncing war and the threat or use of force as means of settling disputes and the maintenance of a Japanese army.

The case of Afghanistan

Whilst I was stationed as Special Representative of the Japanese Government for DDR in Afghanistan, I learned more about unmasking peace with justice. I learned that after September 11 the most effective way for US air raids to defeat the Taliban was to use them to support the Northern Alliance who were fighting on the ground. After the fall of the Taliban, it was the Northern Alliance warlords who became the major obstacle to the stabilisation of Afghanistan. Therefore, the international community was led to believe sustainable peace for Afghanistan was now dependent on defeating these warlords and depleting their military supplies. Here, the importance of Security Sector Reform (SSR) and creating a trustworthy national army, police and judiciary became of paramount importance, and building a single New Afghan Army was most crucial. Japan was responsible for the DDR section. Indeed, the Afghan New Army has been given legitimacy and weapons through the DDR and I was responsible for implementing this strategy.

So, how is the present situation in Afghanistan after DDR? It is getting worse. When I drew up the blueprint to dismantle the Northern Alliance, I clearly warned that disarmament would create a power vacuum. If this power vacuum of the Northern Alliance was *not* filled swiftly by other sectors of SSR, the Taliban might regain power. This power vacuum has not yet been filled; and the coordination among other sectors of SSR seems corrupted. The Police Force, which is the responsibility of Germany, is also problematic. Moreover, the narcotics business is flourishing in Afghanistan feeding corruption at all levels of governance. So, I have to say DDR was a great success as a stand-alone project, but it completely failed in the context of SSR. In other words, DDR was a success politically, but a failure militarily. We have to realise that the Security Sector Reforms of Afghanistan – our strategic response in the so-called war on terror – is collapsing at its very foundations.

In 2009, Operation Enduring Freedom (OEF) is ongoing. The Japanese Self Defense Force has been supporting OEF in the Indian Ocean since 2001 despite ongoing debates about whether to continue this activity. Is there any way out? No, unless the international community closely looks at alternatives to military solutions. There can be no resolution unless we seriously look at governance in Afghanistan, the strongest narcotic nation in the world in spite of all efforts made by the international community. Those former warlords, whom I met through the disarmament program, are still holding immense power as 'mafia' bosses, as well as parliamentarians. The 'collateral' damage caused by OEF has created deep distrust amongst the civilian population towards the international community and the new government.

There can be no resolution unless we link peace with justice. In March 2007, the Amnesty Law was passed in both houses of the Afghan parliament, granting an absolute pardon to any kind of war crimes to anybody, including the top leaders. This was because those former warlords wanted to give themselves further indulgences, preventing their war crimes from being investigated in the future. This resembles the situation in Sierra Leone, where human rights organisations and advocates warned against legitimising 'impunity' as a so-called peaceful solution for conflict.

Approaching peace with justice

There are tensions embedded within the R2P agenda: tensions between prevention and reaction; response and attack; national and international responsibility; and, military intervention as peacekeeping. However, if these tensions can be negotiated in the spirit of working towards a common goal of global security that respects human rights and promotes peace with justice, the Responsibility to Protect (R2P) provides a great opportunity for international citizenship. Of crucial importance is recognition that the absence of violence is not enough to define 'peace'. As seen above in the cases of Sierra Leone and Afghanistan, the international community's intervention to cease direct violence did not include the notion of 'peace with justice', of bringing war criminals to trial rather than rewarding them with government posts. The ensuing negative peace is fragile, unlikely to be sustained. In the case of Iraq, hollow claims about invading the country to instil 'democracy' are equally lacking in an understanding of 'peace with justice'. Unjust military interventions never create 'just peace'. There is a need to be vigilant in reaffirming the language and practice of peace with justice. The global civil society campaign to protect Article 9 of the Japanese Constitution, as detailed in chapter 11, is such an example. Reclaiming R2P as an instrument that promotes peace with justice as a key to global human security is also necessary to any vision of disarmament, demobilisation and rehabilitation towards a nonviolent world.

9

The campaign against US military bases in Australia

Hannah Middleton

The vision of a nonviolent world is not evident in the global map depicting US military bases. The United States has approximately 1000 overseas bases, the largest collection of bases in world history. It includes 268 bases in Germany, 124 in Japan, and 87 in South Korea. Others are scattered around the globe in places like Aruba and Australia, Bulgaria and Bahrain, Colombia and Greece, Djibouti, Egypt, Kuwait, Qatar, Romania, Singapore, and of course, Guantánamo Bay, Cuba. Rather than shrinking, the overseas base network has expanded. Since the invasions of Afghanistan (2001) and Iraq (2003), the United States has created or expanded bases in Uzbekistan, Kyrgyzstan, Tajikistan, Georgia, Qatar, Bahrain, the United Arab Emirates, Oman, and Kuwait. In Iraq and Afghanistan, there may be upwards of 180 installations, respectively, with plans to expand the basing infrastructure in Afghanistan as part of a troop surge.

In Eastern and Central Europe, installations have been created or are in development in Bulgaria, Poland, Romania, and the Czech Republic, and are contributing to rising tensions with Russia. In Africa, as part of the development of the new African Command, the Pentagon has created or investigated the creation of installations in Algeria, Djibouti, Gabon, Ghana, Kenya, Mali, Nigeria, São Tomé and Príncipe, Senegal, and Uganda. The US maintains bases throughout South America and the Caribbean, with the Pentagon exploring the creation of new bases in Colombia and Peru in response to its pending eviction from Manta in Ecuador. In place of big Cold War bases, the Pentagon is focusing on creating smaller and more flexible 'forward operating bases' and even more austere 'lily pad' bases across the so-called arc of instability. Guam and Diego Garcia are facing major expansions.

Historian Chalmers Johnson (2007) says, "America's version of the colony is the military base." In too many recurring cases, soldiers have raped, assaulted or killed local people, especially women. The forced expulsion of the entire Chagossian people to create the secretive base on British colony Diego Garcia in the Indian Ocean is a compelling example. Overseas bases have often heightened military tensions and discouraged diplomatic solutions to international conflicts. Rather than stabilising dangerous regions, overseas bases have often increased global militarisation in an escalating spiral. Overseas bases actually make war more likely, not less.

Military bases invariably discharge toxic waste into local ecosystems, as in Guam where the US military bases have led to no fewer than 19 superfund sites. Such contamination generates resentment and sometimes, as in Vieques in Puerto Rico in the 1990s, full-blown social movements against the bases. The United States used Vieques for live bombing practice 180 days a year, and by the time the United States withdrew in 2003, the landscape was littered with exploded and unexploded ordnance, depleted uranium rounds, heavy metals, oil, lubricants, solvents, and acids. According to local activists, the cancer rate for Vieques was 30 per cent higher than for the rest of Puerto Rico. US military bases infect the planet.

However, the military machine they serve is not impregnable. Organised, persistent, inventive and courageous action has already forced the closure of US bases in the Philippines, Ecuador, Puerto Rico and Kyrgyzstan. More closures require more campaigning. But why campaign against military bases? According to the US Center for Arms Control and Non-Proliferation, total military spending in 2007 was US$1.47 trillion. The United States accounted for 48 per cent of the world's total military spending, while the US and its strongest allies (the NATO countries, Japan, South Korea and Australia) spent $1.1 trillion on their militaries combined, representing 72 per cent of the world's total. In Australia in 2009, military spending had reached $62 million every day and, despite the economic crisis, the Rudd government's Defence White Paper means it will rise to $71 million each and every day. These are enormous amounts which fund a worldwide military leviathan so bloated and complex that peace activists often find it hard to know where to begin their critique.

For the peace activists who formed the anti-bases campaign here in Australia, it was a case of 'grabbing the nearest edge'. The US military facilities on our soil are not an abstract concept – they are radomes (huge white golf balls protecting electronic equipment from nature and surveillance), in the desert, squatting on Aboriginal land, used for spying and fighting. They are something real that we could and can get our teeth into. They are places where we can protest and we have good arguments against them.

It is clear that Australian peace activists cannot stop the United States attacking Iran if that is the path that the Obama administration ultimately chooses. What we can do is to contribute to the worldwide anti-war movement that will inevitably arise if such an attack occurs and, if the Iraq war example persists, even before the bombs begin to fall. More importantly, we can – and have the responsibility to – act to prevent the Australian Government giving political and/or military support to such a move. A key element in such protests would be to reveal the vital role that the US military facilities on Australian soil would play in providing targets, information on terrain and troop movements, surveillance of Iranian communications and much more.

AABCC: establishing the language of nonviolence

The Australian Anti-Bases Campaign Coalition (AABCC) was formed on the basis of research, lobbying and protests that developed over the years from the 1960s when the majority of US bases in Australia were being established. In May 1974, several hundred people travelled to North West Cape from around Australia to protest and occupy the base, "symbolically reclaiming it for the Australian people" (*Builders' labourers' song book* 1975, pp. 190–94). During the occupation, the

Eureka Flag was flown over the base and 55 people were arrested during the protest. Naval Communication Station Harold E. Holt is located on the northwest coast of Australia, six kilometres north of the town of Exmouth, Western Australia. Exmouth was built at the same time as the communications station to provide support to the base and to house dependent families of US Navy personnel.

For a rent of one peppercorn a year, the station provided very low frequency (VLF) radio transmission to United States Navy and Royal Australian Navy ships and submarines in the western Pacific Ocean and eastern Indian Ocean. With a transmission power of 1000 kilowatts, it was the most powerful transmission station in the southern hemisphere. US naval forces were withdrawn in 1993 and the base is currently operated under contract by Boeing Australia, ostensibly as a centre for sun spot surveillance. However, it can be reactivated speedily. This happened at the time of the first Gulf War in 1991 when tourist operators and other businesses occupying buildings on the base site were evicted at 24 hours' notice so naval personnel could move back into the facility. At the trial of Christopher Boyce in 1977, public disclosures by senior ex-Central Intelligence Agency (CIA) employees and research by anti-bases activists provided indisputable evidence of the role of organisations such as the CIA and the National Security Agency (NSA) in the functioning of US bases in Australia.

In Alice Springs a major impetus was given to the campaign by the National Peace Seminar held in 1981. This attracted over 100 participants, and placed the bases issue firmly on the agenda of the peace movement. The women's movement also had a major impact. Inspired by the Greenham Common women's camp in Britain, the Women For Survival peace camp at Pine Gap base in Central Australia in 1983 attracted over 700 women. It was the first action at the base to result in mass arrests and to capture national attention. In 1985, Women for Survival went on to establish a protest camp at Cockburn Sound.

The foundation of the AABCC brought together an extremely diverse group of individuals and organisations. Over 100 groups formally affiliated in the early years, making the coalition the largest peace network in Australia. Affiliates included other peace groups, trade unions, women's and student groups, political parties, environmental organisations, migrant bodies and religious groups. Political, financial and/or organisational support (as opposed to formal affiliation) for the AABCC went wider and deeper.

The AABCC was formally launched in December 1986 at a national conference in Sydney attended by over 250 activists. Always embracing a wide range of interest groups and philosophies and sometimes subject to internal conflicts over policies and tactics, it has nevertheless driven a wide range of nonviolent campaigns including education, lobbying and nonviolent direct actions. Its history reveals some of the strengths and weaknesses of nonviolent forms of protest.

Pine Gap: galvanising a movement for nonviolence

In the early years, the coalition's focus was on the US base at Pine Gap. Officially known as the Joint Defence Space Research Facility, the base is "probably the most important Western intelligence facility in the world" (Professor Des Ball, cited in Stewart 2009) and is one of the largest and most important US satellite ground control stations. Established in 1968 as a CIA intelligence base and situated 19 km south-west of Alice Springs, it consists of a large computer complex with 14 radomes protecting its antennae. Pine Gap is vital for the US military because the satellites it controls span a strategically important third of the globe, encompassing China, southern Russia and the Middle East oil fields.

Pine Gap's most important role is processing information gathered by signals intelligence (SIGINT) satellites and transmitting that information to the United States. These satellites suck up radio transmissions across a wide spectrum. Military intelligence is obtained, along with economic, political and domestic information from national and international telephone and radio communications between allies and enemies alike. Pine Gap's satellites gather military radio transmissions, giving information on military readiness, troop and ship movements and other matters. The satellites can intercept radar emanations, allowing mapping of air defences, anti-ballistic missile radars and early-warning radars. A new satellite system, called SBIRS (Space-Based Infra-Red System), became operational in 2004. This is a key element of the US missile defence project.

A Satellite Relay Ground Station at Pine Gap controls the US Defence Support Program (DSP) early warning satellites. The DSP satellites have infrared sensors which detect the hot exhaust plumes of missiles in their boost phase just after launching. Thus the satellites can provide early warning of a missile attack and also pinpoint the location of the launch sites. They have other functions, including apparently the ability to spy on the phone communications of the Federal Defence Minister (Dorling, Baker & McKenzie 2009).

But Pine Gap was not the only US base to attract the attention of the AABCC. The coalition organised major demonstrations there in 1987 and 2002 but in the intervening years members campaigned against North West Cape (1988); Nurrungar (1989, 1991 and 1993); Smithfield; the Watsonia spy network which includes facilities at Cabarlah, Shoal Bay, Pearce, Harman and Victoria Barracks; the Omega Station in Victoria and NASA tracking stations.

Nurrungar: establishing the practice of nonviolence

During the 1989 protest at Nurrungar Joint Defence Facility (Nurrungar), security was breached at the base when a demonstrator entered one of the radomes. The authorities were so worried that they sent in the army. "Soldiers against 1,000 hippies in a paddock?" one bemused activist asked as we watched the long line of military trucks rumble past. However, it presented us with an opportunity which we seized with delight. We got more publicity for the protest than we had dared hope for, even driving the AFL finals off the front page of the weekend papers! AABCC members then christened themselves as 'the only peace group to bring out the army'.

Nurrungar is situated 15 km south of Woomera in South Australia. During the 1991 protests, a small tent city arose, housing about 1,000 activists with an assortment of buses, vans and cars parked around the edges. The area is beautiful scrubby desert country, full of dust and spiky spinifex clumps. Water was trucked in and latrines dug. The only electricity was for the caravan at the child care area. There were larger tents for healing, media and legal support. It was in this setting that a perennial conflict within the peace movement was argued out – what do we actually mean by the language and practice of nonviolence?

For some activists it is necessary to inform police of the actions they are planning, believing that secrecy is a form of violence. Others believe that a successful action requires secrecy in order to enhance success. For example, it is difficult to trespass on a prohibited area if the police know you are coming and organise to stop you getting in. Some nonviolent activists want to avoid any damage to any property. Others believe that some damage in order to achieve a purposeful activity (such as cutting a fence in order to deliberately trespass) is acceptable so long as the property belongs to the government. Such activists usually argue that damage to the property of an individual citizen is unacceptable. Others believe that damaging property is a cost worth inflicting on an opponent. Fences were not too strongly defended in these debates but damaging police or contractors' vehicles or letting their tyres down provoked sharper disagreements. For some graffiti is a form of property damage and is unacceptable in all circumstances. For others it is 'the peoples' media' and any official or public building is a potential billboard. However, private homes are almost always excluded as acceptable targets.

If activists cross (in whatever way) a boundary line, what then? For some, the idea is to move as quickly as possible towards the base itself with the ultimate aim of getting in and closing it down. For others, a successful protest requires a calm, non-threatening, nonviolent manner. That means skipping and dancing are acceptable, but running is not. For this latter group, it is acceptable to sing, but not to chant slogans or shout. Both groups are critical of the use of abusive language and argue for developing the best possible liaison with the local police officers as an important principled and/or tactical position.

The idea of affinity groups was established as a strategy: that is, autonomous groups of 5–15 people who know each other's strengths and weaknesses and therefore support each other as they participate (or intend to participate) in a nonviolent campaign. Affinity groups allow people to act together in a decentralised and non-hierarchical way by giving decision-making power to the affinity group. The AABCC resolved the divisions about nonviolence by adopting two forms of actions during its peace protests at Nurrungar (and elsewhere). It adopted a broader view of nonviolence (one that allowed secrecy, limited damage to public property for a purposeful activity, etc.) and issued handbooks outlining the principles and asking participants to observe them in all the mass actions organised by the AABCC. It also timetabled actions by affinity groups, indicating the version of nonviolence they had adopted and indicating where others could join the actions providing that they agreed to observe the group's principles. In the vast majority of situations, this pragmatic dual approach was effective.

AABCC: a window of opportunity

The US military bases in Australia proved to be not only the 'nearest edge' but also windows into many other campaigns over the years. These military facilities are connected to so many other major peace issues — from the environment to military spending, from public policy addressing violence against women to Australia's regional security responsibilities, and much more. For example, from the outset the AABCC recognised that the starting point of its struggle is the recognition of the sovereignty of the original inhabitants of this land – the Aboriginal people. The coalition unequivocally supports the campaign for Aboriginal land rights, compensation and self-determination. No AABCC protest is able to take place without prior negotiations with the traditional owners of the land where the action is planned to be staged. For many of us, the visa issued by the Kokatha Peoples' Committee in 1993 allowing us to enter their land to close Nurrungar is a treasured possession.

Recognising the wider regional struggle for independence and self-determination, the AABCC developed links with organisations in the Philippines, South Korea, Belau, Timor Lèste, West Papua, Kanaky, Guam and Hawai'i. A number of solidarity actions took place in the Pacific in October 1986 in support of the demonstrations that occurred throughout Australia against Pine Gap. In the Christmas 1988–89 period, over 100 Australian Anti-Bases activists went to the Philippines to participate in a series of demonstrations against US bases in the Philippines. As part of its Pacific solidarity, the AABCC has organised visits to Australia by indigenous Hawai'ians, the Chamoru from Guam and Native American spokespersons.

In 1991 the AABCC was a major player in demonstrations against Aidex – a giant arms bazaar held in Canberra from 22–28 November. The protest picket/blockade, which was endorsed by the ACT Trades and Labor Council, ensured that the organisers were able to move in their exhibits only with large police escorts and the assistance of club-wielding private security guards. After days of protest, marked by one wedding, many arrests and a number of injuries, long-time activist Denis Doherty called it one of the most violent police operations he has seen. At least two protesters suffered broken arms, one suffered a spinal injury and other injuries included broken wrists, fingers and feet, bruising and abrasions. "This is a much higher rate of injuries than might be expected in most protests," Denis Doherty said at the time. At least one protester was run over, while about 12 were pinned to gates or fences by exhibitors' vehicles.

The protesters made a negotiator available, and she sat in a police station throughout most of the actions. However, the police ignored her except to abuse her, at one point calling her a 'maggot'. After the event was over, a group remained behind to clean up. They lodged complaints with the Commonwealth Ombudsman and the Federal Police Commissioner over police conduct. These complaints included claims that the police fired a flare, pieces of which fell into the camp. The Ombudsman accepted the police story that the flare was fired away from the camp. The protesters also claimed that a police vehicle broadcast machine gun and bomb noises in the vicinity of the camp in the early hours of the morning. The Ombudsman accepted police claims that these noises were made by a generator.

Responding to police claims that the protesters were violent, Denis Doherty said there were different interpretations of nonviolence, but all the protesters stuck to nonviolent tactics. "When you're sitting on the road and you're surrounded by police and you know that if you do anything violent you're going to be totally outnumbered and overpowered, it's crazy to engage in any violence." Another activist commented:

> Things got pretty chaotic at times, and there were good reasons to be angry. Some of the cops appeared to enjoy hurting people. But we were there to protest against the arms race, not to play one-sided games with cops … While we didn't

> stop this Aidex, we probably stopped the next one, and we did help to increase public consciousness about the arms trade and the Australian government's militaristic policies.[1]

These policies are, from time to time, made public in the Australian Government's Defence White Papers, which are major documents outlining strategic assessment and proposed military responses. The AABCC decided that a campaign was necessary to allow the community's voice to be heard on these matters. After all, the policies were supposed to safeguard the Australian people who are also paying for the implementation of such policies. So the *Blue Paper Project* was formed in 1993, describing itself as "an initiative of over 40 non-government organisations to generate discussion of the political and military role Australia will play in the 21st Century, and of the defence philosophy and policies adopted by government" (Middleton 2000). By 2000 the Federal Government found it expedient to introduce, for the very first time, community consultations in the lead up to a new Defence White Paper. The AABCC wrote at that time:

> We need to examine the complex nature of security and the interconnections between its various dimensions and to re-examine our security priorities. Security is becoming more multi-dimensional and it is bad policy to continue to look at defence in isolation. It is time to assess the best way to balance and integrate our responses.
>
> Security is often interpreted to mean military security – the capacity to identify and meet perceived threats to a nation by military means, by the use or the threat of the use of force. Australia's security will be enhanced by attention to social, political and humanitarian issues which affect the people of this country as well as in neighbouring states.
>
> The over-emphasis in casting the military as Australia's guarantee of 'security' has not engendered a true culture of national security. Resources committed to developing the

---

1 Indeed, in February 2009, the AABCC was instrumental with other organisations and individuals in postponing the arms trade bazaar scheduled to take place in Adelaide, South Australia.

military have meant that less is available for constructive work such as preventive diplomacy.

In addition, more money spent on the military means less money for developing strong social cohesion and stability within the nation through employment programs and the health, education and housing needs of Australians and our neighbours.

The most obvious economic feature of military expenditure is its "opportunity costs", that is, the opportunities which are foregone for alternative consumption and investment.

The World Bank has reported that "evidence increasingly points to high military spending as contributing to fiscal and debt crises, complicating stabilisation and adjustment, and negatively affecting economic growth and development".

We cannot afford a continued Cold War paradigm which defines regional engagement as interoperability with the United States in potential high intensity conflicts.

This would require expanding strategic strike and force projection capabilities, maintaining a 'knowledge edge' over regional states and remaining a substantial maritime power. Australia simply cannot afford such an approach economically, politically and socially.

A rational reassessment of our security priorities would lead to a number of conclusions which may be at odds with the Federal Government's stated intention of increasing defence spending … The government's goal must be to minimise military expenditure as far as responsible defence strategy allows. More arms make Australia poorer, not safer (Middleton 2000).

In Sydney in 2000, the tiny minority of peace movement contributors to the public consultation meeting were rudely heckled by the audience and treated with discourtesy by Chairman Andrew Peacock and his staff. A similar community consultation process was put in place in 2008. At that time, as well as developing its own submission, the AABCC undertook a major effort to encourage other groups and individuals to send in submissions and also to attend and speak at the public meetings held around the country. When delivering their comments, in contrast to eight years before, civil society represented the majority of speakers and were listened to with respect and replied to with courteous defensiveness.

Ministerial agreements, however, occur away from the dissenting voice of civil society. At the annual Australian-US Ministerial Consultations (AUSMIN) in Washington in July 2004, Australia and the US agreed to develop a Joint Combined Training Centre which will include state-of-the-art technology that allows commanders to oversee military exercises in real time, then replay missions in debriefs to personnel. Under the concept, facilities will be developed at the Shoalwater Bay Training Area in Queensland and the Bradshaw Training Area and Delamere Air Weapons Range in the Northern Territory at the cost of tens of millions of dollars. The three facilities will be interlinked through a node in the Pacific War Fighting Centre in Hawai'i. Military exercises using the three bases will be directed and monitored by the US military's Pacific Command (PacCom) which is also in Hawai'i. The Tandem Thrust exercises in 1997 and the Talisman Sabre war games in 2005, 2007 and 2009 held in the Shoalwater Bay military training area near Rockhampton are part of this development, sending out a clear message of antagonistic military might.

The AABCC with other groups, especially in Brisbane, have organised protests against these military exercises, preparing fact sheets, sending out media releases, speaking at meetings and film showings and organising buses to travel to Rockhampton. The Peace Convergences have used education, lobbying, media and direct action to educate Australian society about the environmental, social and economic impacts of such 'war games' on their soil. Nonviolent actions have included street marches, music, blockading gates, holding up military convoys, entering the 'war games' area, either openly or secretly to disrupt bombing programs, playing with frisbees on the runway, mass leafleting, public meetings, standing on 'pedestrian crossings' (long strips of cloth painted black and white) on bush roads to prevent tanks passing, street theatre, and much more.

During the Talisman Sabre protests of 2007 (referred to in chapter 3), a group of activists climbed the gate into the prohibited area, taking with them a number of cardboard coffins. They sat in the road, praying and reading out the names of military personnel and civilians killed in the invasion and occupation of Iraq. They were arrested. They were held up as an example to the hundreds of other protestors who had travelled to Rockhampton and, indeed, many regarded their action as moving and powerful. Some went further to suggest that Peace Convergence participants who were not prepared to similarly put their bodies on the line were just 'tourists'. With many activists deeply offended or upset by this, the AABCC made its position public: everyone who came to the protest was to be treated with respect for what they contributed, whatever it was. All we asked was that people came and made their opposition to military exercises manifest.

Over time, anti-bases activists from different countries have networked to get to know each other and share their experiences through face-to-face meetings at conferences and on the web. A view began to develop that expanding and deepening these ad hoc relationships could give support and encouragement to anti-bases campaigns around the world and strengthen the global campaign. The AABCC was an active participant in the preparatory meetings and web-based consultations which led to a conference in 2007 in Quito, Ecuador. Two AABCC representatives joined over 400 other delegates at the meeting which established the International Network Against Foreign Military Bases. The conference included a day-long bus trip from the high mountains to the coast of Ecuador for a large and noisy street march to the US base at the Pacific port of Manta. Set up in 1999 with no public consultation, purportedly to fight the drug trade, the base has been used to sink boats with undocumented immigrants and to support warfare in Colombia. In 2006, Rafael Correa made non-renewal of the base agreement part of his presidential campaign. When he was elected, the community held him to his promise, and a constituent assembly inserted a ban on all foreign military presence in the new constitution of Ecuador.

Promoting weapons, destabilising communities: protesting weapons, stabilising communities

Similarly, the AABCC has been in the forefront of education and protests against the increasing involvement of Australia in the US missile defence project. Over the past 30 years, the AABCC has witnessed the US planning to militarise, commercially exploit and to control space, taking corporate globalisation to a new and more terrifying level. The spin is that the US military push into space is about 'missile defence'. However, the US military explicitly says it wants to 'control' space to protect its economic interests and establish superiority over the world. "With regard to space dominance, we have it, we like it and we're going to keep it," said Keith Hall, Assistant Secretary of the Air Force for Space.

Vision for 2020, a 1996 report of the United States Space Command (USSC), proclaims that its mission is "dominating the space dimension of military operations to protect US interests and investment." A century ago, "[n]ations built navies to protect and enhance their commercial interests" by ruling the seas, the report says. Now it is time to rule space. The USSC's 1998 *Long Range Plan* underlines the globalisation aspect of US space war plans, saying, "[w]idespread communications will highlight disparities in resources and quality of life – contributing to unrest in developing countries … The gap between 'have' and 'have-not' nations will widen, creating regional unrest" (USSC 1998). By controlling space and the Earth below, the US intends to keep those 'have-nots' in line.

Bruce Gagnon, coordinator of the Global Network Against Weapons and Nuclear Power In Space, says the program has "never been about defence. It's always been about controlling space, dominating space, denying other countries access to space and the US being the master of space. And that isn't a defensive posture" (Grossman 2002).

However, he also points out that:

Spending hundreds of billions of dollars on Star Wars will take money away from education, programmes for women and children, and health care. There is a direct link between promoting weapons for space and the destabilisation of our communities. People must connect these struggles (Grossman 2002).

References

Builders' labourers' song book (1975). Camberwell, Vic: Widescope International in association with the Australian Building Construction Employees' and Builders' Labourers' Federation.

Dorling, P., Baker, R. & McKenzie, N. (2009). How Defence officials spied on Fitzgibbon. *The Canberra Times*, 26 March, Australia. Retrieved from www.canberratimes.com.au/news/national/national/general/how-defence-officials-spied-on-fitzgibbon/1470418.aspx.

Grossman, K. (2002). Star Wars: protecting globalization from above. *CorpWatch*, 18 January. Retrieved from www.corpwatch.org/article.php?id=1333.

Johnson, C. (2007). *Nemesis: the last days of the American republic (American Empire Project)*. New York: Metropolitan Books.

Middleton, H. (2000). Comments on Defence Review 2000. Blue Paper Project website. Retrieved from www.anti-bases.org/blue_paper/commentsondefence.htm.

Stewart, C. (2009). Block on Chinese mining bid 'linked to Pine Gap'. *The Australian*, 2 April.

United States Space Command (USSC) (1996). *Vision for 2020*. Retrieved from www.fas.org/spp/military/docops/usspac/visbook.pdf.

USSC (1998). *Long range plan*, April. Retrieved from www.fas.org/spp/military/docops/usspac/lrp/toc.htm.

10

The road to Fallujah[1]

Donna Mulhearn

April 2004 Fallujah

Driving through the empty streets of Fallujah, I felt the stench of death in the air. I could feel the terror of the families locked behind the closed doors. Already 700 dead. The graveyards were full, so the local soccer field had to be dug up to make room to bury the dead from the assault on this town.

We cautiously made our way through the deserted streets straight to the clinic where our friends had helped out a few days before – a small neighbourhood clinic that had been transformed into a makeshift hospital after the main hospital in Fallujah was closed to locals by the US military. Weary staff adapted admirably to the constant influx of wounded delivered in the backs of cars, vans and pick-ups – extra beds were wheeled in and cans of soft drink were emptied from the Coke machine so it could be used to cool bags of blood.

But the clinic had no disinfectant, no anaesthetic, and lacked much of the other vital equipment required for the type of surgery the horrific wounds demanded. And as a form of collective punishment all electricity to Fallujah had been cut for days. The clinic had a generator, but when the petrol ran out the doctors had to continue surgery using the glow from cigarette lighters, candles and torches.

---

1 A version of this chapter was first published in *Griffith REVIEW* 17: *Staying Alive* (August 2007).

We spoke to the doctors – they were exhausted, and looked defeated as they told us the stories of their recent cases: a ten-year-old boy with a bullet wound to the head from US snipers, a grandmother with abdominal bullet wounds, young men with severe burns, limbs blown off, and so on. Each time a new patient arrived, the doctors quickly got up, donned a new set of surgical gloves and got to work. Many had laboured twenty-four hours straight, others regularly survived on only a few hours' sleep for days at a time. They didn't complain. They are the heroes of Fallujah.

We asked how we could help. The doctors asked if we could accompany an ambulance packed with food and medical supplies across town to a clinic in the US-controlled section of the town which could not receive aid because of constant sniper fire. The doctors figured our foreign nationality could make a difference in negotiating with the soldiers the safe passage of the ambulance.

It might seem a strange and unnecessary mission to help an ambulance drive from one place to another – anywhere else in the world, it's a basic right. But this is Fallujah and this is war, and nothing is as it should be – despite guarantees laid out in the Geneva Conventions. The last time an ambulance went to this part of town it was shot at by US troops. I know this because two of my friends were in that ambulance, trying to reach a pregnant woman in premature labour. They didn't reach her, but the bullet holes in the ambulance are proof they tried.

So we packed the ambulance with supplies and got in the back. With me were three other foreigners: Jo, Dave and Beth – two British, an American and an Aussie, a good representation of young people from the 'coalition of the willing' trying to counterbalance our countries' military intervention with loving intervention. We donned bright blue surgical gowns and held our passports in our hands. A couple of medical staff were with us in the back, and the drivers were up the front.

We drove slowly through the parts of Fallujah controlled by Iraqi fighters then stopped in a side street that faced a main road. We could not go any further; the main road was under watch and control of US snipers who had a habit of shooting at anything that moved. We parked the ambulance in the side street and the four of us got out with the mission to approach the American soldiers, communicate with them and get permission for the ambulance to continue to the clinic.

The area was completely quiet. The silence was unnerving. We prepared the loudspeaker, put our hands in the air and held our passports high. Before we ventured onto the main road, we called out a message from the side street. "Hello? American soldiers, we are a group of international aid workers. We are unarmed. We are asking permission to transport an ambulance full of medical supplies to the clinic across the way. Can you give us safe passage?"

The reply was a chilling silence.

We repeated the message. Again silence.

We looked at each other. Perhaps the soldiers were too far away to hear us? We had no choice but to walk on to the main road and hope that we would be clearly visible as unarmed civilians. I took a deep breath and for a split second thought that this was probably the most dangerous thing I had ever done. I looked at the others and could tell we were all thinking the same thing: "If we don't do this, who will?" Our white Western privilege meant our lives were considered more valuable than Iraqi lives, and we had to try to use this privilege, as obscene as it is.

The courage of the others inspired me as we all stepped out onto the road together. We walked slowly with our arms raised. My eyes scanned the tops of the buildings for snipers. We didn't know where they were, so we walked in the direction of the clinic. We repeated the message over and over again on the loudspeaker. In the silence, it would have been heard for hundreds of metres. It echoed eerily through the neighbourhood.

I turned my head briefly and just in time. In the distance, I saw two white flashes, then heard the loud, staccato "bang, bang" of gunshots and rapidly realised they were shooting in our direction. It all happened so fast: hearing the whizz of the bullets just above our heads, ducking, diving for cover against a wall.

In the scramble, I fell. My hands broke my fall on to sharp gravel on the rough ground. I felt the sting of pain and could see the blood, but I had no time to stop and check what had happened. We ended up in someone's backyard, and then made our way back to the ambulance, jumping fences and going through gates. My hands were covered with blood, my left foot cut and my passport stained red, an indelible reminder of the episode.

We regrouped. Although shocked and shaken, we didn't want to give up. Now we knew where the soldiers were, we could walk towards them. We decided to go out again. Same drill: we called out the message, then stepped out on to the road – this time facing the direction of the gunfire. "Hello! American soldiers. We are foreign aid workers – British, Australian, American. We are not armed. We are asking permission to transport an ambulance on this road."

My injured hand was shaking as I held my passport, now damp with blood. I tried to work out what I was feeling – fear, anger, determination? I still don't know. We had only repeated the message twice and walked a few metres when our answer came. Two more bullets shaved the top of our heads. I entered a state of shock. I had been shot at not once, but twice, by American soldiers after politely asking permission to transport aid to a hospital. Their persistent warning shots meant the answer was a firm "No".

We stepped back to the corner, but Jo was furious and continued on the loud speaker. "Do you know it is a breach of the Geneva Conventions to fire at unarmed civilians and at ambulances?" she cried. "How would you feel if your sister was under siege without food or water?"

We took the loudspeaker from her but not before she conveyed one more message. "May your trigger finger be plagued with warts!" She continued several other curses under her breath.

We headed back to the clinic. My head was spinning. I felt angry, frustrated, my hands were aching. But strangely enough my spirit was intact. We had just walked with our hands in the air like vulnerable lambs into the face of armed soldiers, yet this nonviolent action and my complete and utter faith that the 'rightness' of the mission would protect me had been immensely empowering.

Silent victims

That afternoon, on the footpath outside the clinic, I saw one of the saddest sights of war. It was a small boy, about ten years old. He'd just got out of a van that was used to transport the wounded and dead. The disturbing thing was not that he was wounded. On the contrary – he had collected the bodies and was driving the van! He unloaded the bodies, reported the stories to the doctors and onlookers and gave orders while casually holding a Kalashnikov in his hand as if it were a cricket bat. It wasn't a cricket bat, but I couldn't stop thinking that it should have been. With a scarf wrapped around his neck, a strong face and confident attitude, I could see he was an experienced fighter. My heart sank at the thought of this little boy, now a little Mujahadeen, playing with bullets instead of marbles. The locals said he was a good shot.

It got worse. I saw a cute little girl, with pigtails, a pink shirt and a polka-dot scarf, also about ten years old, also brandishing a Kalashnikov. It was almost as big as her, but she handled it with ease. I hoped that she didn't really use it. I hoped she had dolls at home to play with. A woman explained that the girl had lost her parents and was now the guardian of her younger siblings. "She had no choice but to protect them. What do you expect?" the woman asked. Children, whether wounded, killed, traumatised by bombing or prematurely recruited as soldiers or family protectors, are the silent victims of war.

Captured

We agreed that if there was nothing more we could do, we should hit the road, aware it would be a difficult and dangerous drive out of the Fallujah city limits. It was unclear which group controlled what road, so our driver had to choose the route wisely.

It seems he didn't. We drove to the edge of town and headed towards a lonely, dusty road. The quietness was ominous and suddenly gunshots ripped through the air coming from all directions. We were caught in crossfire.

Dave grabbed the steering wheel and with his head down somehow managed to reverse the car, turn it around and slowly head back towards the town. He was driving with one hand on the wheel, his eyes just peeping over the dashboard. We three girls were in the back huddled together with our heads on each other's laps.

When we thought we were out of danger of flying bullets, we slowly raised our heads.

"Hello?" A group of heavily armed Iraqi fighters, commonly referred to here as Mujahadeen, were standing on the road, waiting for us. We had driven straight into their camp.

At first I was relieved: "Thank God we got out of the crossfire." But then I noticed a man whose face I couldn't see, because of the scarf wrapped around his head, aiming a rocket-launcher at me – well, it was aimed at everyone, but it felt like it was just me. It was a long shiny metal thing that protruded from his shoulder. Then I noticed that our car was surrounded by the scarved men, all their weapons pointing at us.

Next we did what came by instinct – put our hands in the air to indicate our lack of arms and willingness to cooperate. They motioned for us to get out of the car. I noticed Emad, our translator, had raced back and was speaking to them in Arabic, explaining who we were and what we were doing.

I was hopeful that Emad would get us out of trouble, but this group of fighters didn't know him and didn't know who we were, and they needed to check us out. To them, we could well have been coalition spies. They put us into another car, and we drove through the deserted town.

At this stage I didn't feel that I had been captured – I figured they'd just check out our story and give us a cup of tea and we'd be on our way. I'm not the panicky type – and remained calm as I got into their car, happy that the guy with the rocket launcher could no longer point it at me. I tried to ignore the fact that the driver had a grenade resting between his legs.

When we got to the house, they offered us water and I heard Emad say: "Take it, you don't know when you'll get any again."

"What?" I thought, still hoping for tea, but accepting the water in case Emad was right. We sat on the floor and before long they brought in some heavily armed warrior-type fighters who were obviously the leaders of this particular militia. The head guy was dressed in khaki and had a long, shiny rocket flung across his shoulder as if it were a golf club. He was a heavy-duty Rambo-type.

Under guard, we were driven to another house. "That cup of tea will come as soon as we get inside," I thought, my spirits rising again. We were ushered into a large room lined with cushions on the floor – a typical Iraqi living room, although it felt like a family had not sat in there for a long time. We sat on the floor waiting for instructions. A man sat near the door holding a gun, making it clear that we were not free to leave.

After a while, an older man came in dressed in civilian clothes – a long, brown, traditional dress. He seemed like an 'elder' type, a leader in the community. He had a serious face, but it was also gentle. It became clear that it was his job to figure out who we were. When it was pointed out that I was Australian he raised his eyebrows. He decided to interrogate me first and the others were taken out of the room.

The following thirty minutes of interrogation took me through a range of emotions. I felt profoundly sad, ashamed to the point of anguish, angry, passionate and at one point moved to tears. At the end I was shaken and could hardly talk. Not because of fear of this man or his group, but from the shocking realisation of how deeply hurt and betrayed he felt – betrayed by my country.

Interrogation

The man in the long, brown dress was fascinated by Australia's involvement in the war. But he was also deeply disappointed. "Tell me about this man, your president … Howard?" he asked. "Why did he go to war with Iraq?"

Then, referring to the then Prime Minister's remarks in the media confirming Australia's commitment to keeping troops in Iraq, he asked: "Why did he appear on the television pledging support for America?"

Howard's comments were given extensive coverage on Iraqi TV and Arab satellite networks such as Al-Jazeera. My Iraqi friends back in Baghdad were alarmed when they saw this, and warned that it could land me in trouble. "Donna, what is he doing? Tell this man to keep his mouth shut! He will make all Iraqis hate Australia. You must stay inside now!" one friend warned me.

As I tried to reason with the brown man, I felt that I had the weight of Australian foreign policy resting on my shoulders. The load was heavy. And this burden was the last thing I needed while being held captive by Iraqi fighters from Fallujah who felt the full brunt of the invasion every day. I cursed John Howard in my head. Why couldn't he come and explain to the Iraqi people why he had participated in an invasion of their country? How could I even attempt to explain a policy that I believed was reckless, small-minded, dangerous and irresponsible?

I didn't. I told the man I didn't agree with John Howard, so I could not justify his decision. For the next few minutes, I put forward my views on the war with as much passion and clarity as I could muster sitting on the floor in that dark room in a Fallujah house. I explained that I came to Iraq last year as a human shield to show my opposition to war and violence, and to be with the Iraqi people in solidarity. And now I had returned to help pick up the pieces – especially the pieces of the broken children left homeless and suffering trauma as a result of the war. I explained that John Howard was a conservative politician, and that I supported parties that opposed him. That we were hopeful the upcoming elections would deliver us a new prime minister who would withdraw Australian troops from Iraq.

His face brightened. "A new prime minister?"

"We hope for this," I said.

"*Insha' Allah* (God willing)," he replied.

Finally, I'd made a connection that may well have saved me. But still, with pain in his eyes, the brown man's questions continued and became more specific. "How many Australian soldiers are in Iraq? Where are they based and what are they doing? What do the Australian people think about Iraq? Do they want to be at war with Iraq?" He looked intently at me: "Do Australians want to hurt Iraqi people?"

The question broke my heart and I had to choke back tears as I thought about all my friends at home who opposed the war. I told him that Australians didn't want to hurt Iraqi people. That the majority opposed the war and took to the streets in their hundreds of thousands the previous year in demonstrations. "Then why did the government go to war, if the people didn't agree? This is what happened, and *you* want to bring *us* democracy?"

I was back to square one, shrugging my shoulders and feeling stupid that I came from a so-called democracy. I wanted to cry. I wanted to scream. I wanted to express to him the longings of every Australian man, woman and child who marched and took action opposing the war. I wanted him to feel their desire for peace. I desperately wanted him to believe this. I said it as best I could.

He sat back and thought for a few moments. I sat in silence in my anguish.

The silence was broken by gunshots and explosions. Outside on the streets of Fallujah, where bodies of women and children lie on the ground, outside where an ambulance cannot move without being shot at, outside where no one can walk freely without the risk of a sniper's bullet through the head.

I was held in a room with a man holding a gun blocking the door, but in that moment I realised that I was not the captive. He was. And his wife and his children and his neighbours … I hung my head in shame. I couldn't hold the tears any longer so I let them come. Tears for Iraq and for Australia.

After the brown man finished questioning all of us, he searched our bags. This was good for us because he looked at our cameras. The most recent pictures and footage showed images of what we did in Fallujah and our work with the children back in Baghdad. With the search complete, he left; but an armed guard sat near the door. We sat on the floor and talked as the afternoon passed, trying to stay positive. Jo, who has worked as a clown in Iraq, got out her balloons and made a couple of balloon animals. She gave one to the man with the gun. "Do you have children?" she asked him.

"Yes," he said. "They've been taken to Baghdad." She handed him a purple giraffe for them which made him smile. Then he began to talk. "They killed my brother," he said softly. "And my brother's son and my sister's son. My other brother is in jail. I am the only one left. Do you know how this feels?"

The looks on our faces told him we didn't.

"And now my best friend was killed. His throat was cut by American soldiers after they shot him in the leg. He was on the street and couldn't run away."

"Oh God," I thought. His friend was no doubt one of the bodies that had come into the clinic. As this man's anguish gushed out of him I wondered if he wanted to whack us all as revenge for the death of half his family. Or perhaps that would not be enough to relieve his pain. But, in an act of restraint I dearly wished others had shown, he didn't. He didn't punish us for something *we* didn't do, despite the fact he and his family had been punished for something *they* didn't do. As if to read our minds, he reminded us: "We are Muslims. We won't hurt you." Then he just held the purple giraffe and sat in silence.

They brought us a big meal and some tea (yes it came!). Hours passed in the windowless room then we were moved to another house.

Inside the new house, we girls were put into a room while David was kept separate. After an hour or so, there was a knock at the door. The man had a message: "Tomorrow you will be released and taken to Baghdad. We must arrange for someone to take you there," he said. "The roads are dangerous and you could be kidnapped."

We smiled with irony at the concern of our captors. When he closed the door, the others cheered and we all hugged each other. He told us we would leave after first prayers, at dawn. They gave us an evening meal and more tea and biscuits.

The next day as we approached the road out of Fallujah, there were scores of cars in a long queue waiting to leave the city, but not moving. Our hearts sank. Would we be stuck another night? Our driver wove his way up to the top of the queue. The people there explained that American soldiers had blocked the road and were not letting anyone pass. They had just fired shots at one car that had attempted to leave using the road. One lady pointed to her car full of children. "I want to take my children out of here before they're killed," she said. "Why won't they let us leave?"

I looked at the other cars: they were all packed with families, desperate to escape the bloody violence of Fallujah. There were hundreds of them. I couldn't believe the soldiers would not let these people drive to safety. "Can you help us?" the people pleaded.

We looked at each other and decided we had to try. We got out of the car and prepared ourselves. There was a long stretch of empty road that was the 'no man's land' between cars and the soldiers. We held our hands in the air, grabbed the loudspeaker and began to walk down the deserted road towards the concrete and razor wire where the soldiers were. The blood on my passport reminded me of the last time I did this. We hoped for a better outcome this time.

The roadblock

So we began to walk down the empty, dusty road towards a collection of concrete blocks and razor wire where the soldiers were guarding the roadblock. Behind us was a queue of hundreds of cars full of ordinary people – terrified and trying to flee to safety. A few had already given up and turned around after gunshots from US soldiers warned them not to come any closer. Fallujah had become a bloody prison – no one was allowed in or out.

We couldn't see the soldiers, but we followed the same procedure as we had a few days before: *hijabs* off so it was clear we were Western, arms in the air, passport in hands and message on the loudspeaker: "Hello American soldiers. We are unarmed foreign civilians. We are trying to leave Fallujah – please don't shoot."

We repeated this a few times and walked slowly towards the checkpoint. I squinted into the distance as I heard our message echo back, but there was no movement ahead. We were halfway down the road when finally I saw the outline of a soldier in the distance. We repeated the message and heard his faint reply: "We won't shoot. Proceed."

Relieved, we walked the rest of the way to meet him. He was surprised to see us, and a little on edge, but greeted us cordially. About ten others hovered around with machine guns in hand, bemused by the sight of us. We explained that we had been in Fallujah to help deliver and distribute aid and that we were trying to get back to Baghdad. The soldier in charge agreed to let our two cars pass. That was great news, but it was not enough. "What about the others?" we asked – the "others" being the hundreds of families sitting in their hot, overcrowded cars hoping somehow to escape the hell that had descended. Anxious women, frightened children, crippled old men and young men who didn't want to fight. "You must let these people through," we pleaded. "They just want to travel to safety."

The solider in charge hesitated.

"They are civilians with a few belongings just wanting to escape the violence," we explained. We put the case for another five minutes or so and finally the soldier responded.

"Okay, we'll let the women and children through," he announced as though he'd made a great concession – a concession that was useless. This soldier didn't seem to have a grip on local culture.

"The women don't drive cars. And if one or two of them do they can't go alone without the company of a man from their family," I told him gently. His concession meant that none of the hundreds of cars in the queue would be able to pass.

He nodded: "Okay, we'll let the old men through."

Again, this would have allowed just a few cars to pass. I didn't understand the logic in forcing the young men to stay, and questioned him. "The men who want to leave don't want to fight you – surely you want to let them go so they are not forced to pick up a gun to defend themselves against you?"

The soldier in charge didn't respond out loud, but one of the others did, perhaps not meaning for us to hear. "We want them all in there together so we can finish them off all at once. It makes it easier."

I would have taken this as a joke had the soldier in charge not reiterated his command immediately. "No. The men cannot leave. We have orders."

We headed back to the queue. The people were waiting for us, their faces hopeful. A translator explained: "The woman and children can go, and the old men."

A clean-cut man in his forties standing near me grabbed my arm. He held his baby daughter in his arms. "Can I go?" he asked with desperation. My heart sank. I had to explain to this Iraqi man with his baby, wife and car full of kids that he could not leave the bombing, the shooting, the chaos of Fallujah on a public road that belonged to him.

A tank from a foreign country which had come with claims of 'liberation' was taking this man's freedom before my eyes. I put my head down.

"No," I said. "They won't let you go." I hardly believed the words as I spoke them. "They will let your wife and children go," I said, knowing how stupid that would sound to him.

"How can they go alone?" he screamed pointing to the empty driver's seat where he would have to sit for his family to escape to safety. The fear on his wife's face crushed my heart. I couldn't take it anymore, couldn't bear to see these families turn back to God knows what.

We headed back to the soldiers to try again. We told them the cars were all driven by men with their families. Not allowing them to pass would mean refusing women and children a passage to safety. "Do you know the Geneva Convention?" we asked, not really expecting an answer. The head guy shuffled from foot to foot as he deliberated. We stood holding our breaths with our fingers crossed.

"Okay," he said. "Men can pass, but only if they are accompanying a family." Yes! That would at least ensure the women and children could get out, and many of the men. We went back and explained the new condition. For people who couldn't hear, we just pointed to their car and gave a thumbs up. They clapped, cheered and yelled out: "Thank you! God bless you!"

But it was a bitter-sweet victory – tempered by the fact that the only reason the soldiers allowed anyone through was because a bunch of foreigners were watching and reminding them of the Geneva Conventions. They should have just let them through because they were Iraqi people wanting to move about in their own country. I shuddered to think what was happening at other checkpoints. And still there were the young men. There was a large group in their early twenties in the back of a pick-up. They would not leave Fallujah today. We could not give them a logical reason and did not repeat to them the threatening words of the soldiers.

So we got back into our cars and slowly led the way through no man's land towards the checkpoint. They searched our cars and we were ushered through. The car behind us, packed with a large family, got through too. They stuck close behind us. I turned my head to check what was happening. The soldiers were doing thorough searches of the cars. It would be a long day for these Fallujans, but hopefully they would eventually drive to safety. As for the young men who didn't want to fight

– they would have to go back to the hell of Fallujah and face the uncertainty of being a civilian caught in a war where there were no rules.

As we drove away, I was overcome by sadness as I remembered the fear and desperation on the faces of the people. I couldn't help thinking: why should these people be so frightened that they are forced to flee their own homes? Why are they now refugees in their own country? Where would they go? How long will their lives be upside down? How long before the killing would stop and promised 'freedom' would come?

There were no answers as we drove away to the sound of another bomb blast shaking Fallujah.

11

The floating peace village: an experiment in nonviolence

Yoshioka Tatsuya

It was 1983 when a group of university friends began the project Peace Boat – a floating peace village. Twenty-five years later, Peace Boat is a recognised Japan-based, international NGO that works to promote peace and sustainability through the organisation of global voyages onboard a large passenger ship. Each voyage takes up to 1000 people from all walks of life for three months calling to an average of twenty countries. On board, participants attend various peace education programs such as the Global University and while in ports, we interact with the local people to share cultural exchange programs and joint cooperation activities. These activities are carried out on a partnership basis with other civil society organisations and communities around the world.

Our original motivation was the controversy over the revision of history textbooks in Japan in the early 1980s. As university students at the time, we all felt a great sense of crisis due to the misleading historical texts about the Japanese army's invasions throughout the Asia-Pacific region and Japan's actions during World War II. Those of us standing on the side of the historical perpetrators of violence prefer to forget about these truths, and a decisive gap in historical recognition develops between us and those standing on the other side of history – those whose lands were invaded and will never be able to forget the violence. In our view, this would render eventual reconciliation and the establishment of true friendly relations impossible.

Peace Boat in the 1980s: the Asia-Pacific

With the slogan of 'reflect upon past wars, create peace for the future', we chartered a passenger ship, gathered several hundred students and citizens and started to run peace voyages throughout the Asia-Pacific region once or twice a year, for between two and three weeks at a time. On board these voyages were also NGO activists and specialists on peace, human rights and environmental issues from both Japan and the country visited. The main purpose of these voyages was to consider past conflicts and work towards reconciliation for the Asia-Pacific region through the creation of new relationships. These voyages became the organisation we now call Peace Boat.

In the early days, we spent a large proportion of time visiting places which had been invaded by the Japanese army. For example, we visited the site of the Nanjing Massacre in China; places where many Australian and British prisoners of war lost their lives such as the sites of the Thai-Burma Railway and the Death March of the Philippines' Bataan Peninsula and Sakhalin where many Koreans were abandoned.

However, this focus on the past developed into a concern about contemporary international issues of the 1980s. We began to work also on educating for the peace and justice issues surrounding the Vietnam War; massacres under the Pol Pot Regime; the Sino-Vietnamese War; and other conflicts in Asia, including the Cold War as it was experienced in the region. Furthermore, we became involved in the independence movement of Timor L'este, a regional neighbour also invaded at one time by the Japanese army.

Peace Boat's third voyage in 1985 visited Vietnam for the first time – a country then under the Cold War socialist system. Two days after departing from Ho Chi Minh City after having enjoyed exchange with local youth, the ship came across a boat carrying over twenty refugees who had fled from Vietnam, only to have their boat's engine fail and to have been floating without food and water for over two weeks. Meeting these people risking their lives to escape from the very Vietnam which had so warmly welcomed Peace Boat just two days earlier was a great shock – where was the 'liberation' and 'socialism' we had heard so much about? To add to that question, the voyage also visited Manila, then in the midst of the Marcos dictatorship. Although hearing about the freedom of capitalism in the Philippines, Peace Boat participants came face-to-face with people living as garbage collectors at Smokey Mountain. Seeing these radically different situations in two South-East Asian nations opened our eyes to the fact that North-South issues were even more serious than the East-West issues of the Cold War – namely, the gaps between the wealthy and the poor. Poverty was a peace issue too. We came to realise that just as the North-South issue can be seen in Japan and South-East Asia, it is also a problem of North, Central and South America; of Europe and Africa and the Middle East. Similar North-South structures exist all over the world. Without linking these different places, we will not be able to see the fundamental core of peace with justice problems.

These experiences in Asia in the mid-1980s, the subsequent democracy movement in Eastern Europe, the end of the Cold War, the violence at Tiananmen Square and the collapse of the Soviet Union were decisive influences on the evolution of Peace Boat. These major conflicts made us re-acknowledge that issues in the Asia-Pacific cannot be resolved only within this region. Furthermore, the collapse of the East-West Cold War structures underscored the North-South divide, leading to the recognition that resolution of conflicts regarding human security would only be possible through global actions.

The Global Summit held in Brazil's Rio de Janeiro in 1992 also had a great influence on the Peace Boat's agenda. The issue of the global environment and sustainable development as a key human security concern was acknowledged by the international community. Since its beginnings, Peace Boat has acknowledged the significance of environmental issues, which are inherently important to realising peace for the world. For example, in Vietnam we learned about the lingering effects of Agent Orange and other defoliants and in Borneo we conducted studies on the destruction of the rainforest.

Thus, it was a natural progression for us to begin global voyages in 1990. Since then, Peace Boat has circumnavigated the globe over fifty times. From visits to Eastern Europe in the early stages of democracy and Russia in the days after the collapse of the Soviet Union, to direct association with conflict regions including Palestine and Israel; Bosnia, Croatia and Kosovo in the former Yugoslavia; Cyprus; Northern Ireland; the Basque region; Eritrea, Algeria and Mozambique in Africa; and Nicaragua, El Salvador and Colombia in Latin America, we have been able to deepen direct exchange with the local communities and members of local NGOs, creating dialogue for a peaceful, sustainable, global society.

Peace education: steering the Peace Boat

Peace Boat's Global University program is held on board the three-month voyages at sea. The comprehensive peace education program that forms Global University includes workshops and seminars held by a wide range of specialists and activists from around the world, field work and exposure tours to visit the actual places studied while in port, and direct networking and campaigning activities on board the ship and beyond. The Global University combines theory and practice of nonviolence via study, experience, networking and action, to create a 'peace university' while living in this 'floating peace village'.

A particularly unique aspect of this program is that Peace Boat itself is a community – which I refer to as a 'village'. Throughout the relatively long three-month semester onboard, students share their living space with teachers, resource persons, instructors and the broader onboard community. The development of these personal relationships underpins the educational pedagogy inherently built into the study environment itself; that is, 'coexisting with others' as one of the most important aspects to the realisation of peace.

Educating for peace includes enabling safe, creative spaces to engage cross-cultural learning, often between conflicting parties. Peace Boat voyages are a moving space which can link people throughout the world. For example, a representative of a Peruvian NGO supporting people living in slums joined the ship to visit El Salvador; there he learned about building cost-effective eco-toilets with natural materials and, upon his return to Peru, was able to use this idea to improve hygiene in the slums.

A women's peace conference planned by a group of Colombian women from all strata of society, which could not be held in the country itself due to the ongoing conflict, was held onboard the ship as a neutral, safe space for dialogue. Through direct exchange in ports and international solidarity actions, Peace Boat is able to create a physical and real space for networking that transcends national borders.

This is embodied in the International Students Programme, through which we invite youth from regions in conflict to join the ship. The project aims to empower its participants to seek peaceful dialogues to the conflicts in which their communities and countries are involved. Over the years, students from Palestine and Israel, the former Yugoslavia, India and Pakistan, the US, Colombia, Brazil, Argentina, Chile, Eritrea, Turkey and Greece, and the East-Asian nations of Korea, China and Taiwan have all joined the ship and participated in these conflict transformation programs, ranging from a week to a full three-month global voyage.

The program has had a significant impact on the lives of participants, for example that of a young Palestinian and a young Israeli who, having struggled to resolve their differences and build trust through their experiences on board, went on to initiate a joint project to build peace once they returned to their homes. In October of 2003, their joint initiative was recognised for its achievements in bringing young Israelis and Palestinians together for dialogue and was awarded the Mount Zion Award from a Jerusalem foundation. Additionally, despite the tremendous obstacles posed by the ongoing Israeli Occupation and the deteriorating situation on the ground in Palestine, the two have continued to cooperate and have travelled to Japan on a national speaking tour to raise awareness about peace with justice concerns in the Middle East.

'Peace and Green Boat' project – partnerships with Korea

Korea, as Japan's closest neighbour, and also arguably its biggest colonial victim, has always had a special focus in our activities. This is particularly because Peace Boat's founding members were active participants in the Korean Democracy solidarity movement as students.

Even now, more than sixty years after the end of World War II, there are deep tensions between the Korean Peninsula and Japan. These tensions are rooted in various unresolved issues, such as political relations between Japan and the North of the Korean peninsula, which remain an open wound. Indeed, I believe that North-East Asia is still dangerously fractured along Cold War lines, and the effects of this frigid relationship on security, the economy and civil society cannot be overlooked as East Asia works towards consolidating and building closer international relations. It is imperative that people take action at the grassroots level to try to build cooperation and trust based on mutual respect and understanding.

Peace Boat has organised numerous regional voyages to the Korean peninsula, including two historic cruises that visited both sides of the divided peninsula within the same voyage. On each visit to the north of the peninsula, we have engaged in reconciliation and dialogue activities with groups including students, former forced labourers and Korean victims of the atomic bombing of Japan.

As our region is traditionally weak in respect for civil society activity, these programs have benefited tremendously from the example set by South Korean civil society. Peace Boat has certainly learned a great deal from our partners in Seoul. We have thus been delighted to forge a partnership with South Korea's 'Green Foundation', a project through which we are jointly launching a ship on a regional voyage for peace every year for ten years. The first of such 'Peace and Green Boats', Peace Boat's fiftieth Voyage for Peace, was entitled 'Peace and Green in Asia – Towards A Common Vision of the Future for East Asia'. The 2005 voyage marked the sixtieth anniversary of the end of World War II and the fortieth anniversary of the normalisation of diplomatic relations between Korea and Japan.

The experience of coordinating a voyage with responsibility shared equally between Korea and Japan has proved to be a powerful catalyst for dialogue and cooperation, and has led to moving person-to-person links between the people of the two countries, which despite being so close geographically, are still far apart. The 'Peace and Green Boat' project is a concrete step by civil society to strengthen peaceful relations in East Asia.

Global Partnership for the Prevention of Armed Conflict (GPPAC)

Entering the twenty-first century, we were struck with a huge shock – the September 11 attacks and the following wars in Afghanistan and Iraq. Particularly significant was the Iraq War, in which the governments of the United Kingdom and Japan amongst others supported the Bush administration in its neglect of both international law and the international community to wage war. Here, the Peace Boat provided a unique space for nonviolent action as we used it as a moving billboard to actively protest against the war, and also as a vehicle to transport wheelchairs, beds and medical supplies to a hospital in Iraq. The realities of the Iraq War have also made clear to us – in a cruel and horrific way – the urgent need for stronger global networks to build peace.

With this in mind, Peace Boat became involved in a new undertaking, as a member of the International Steering Group of the Global Partnership for the Prevention of Armed Conflict (GPPAC). This global partnership was established as a response to former United Nations Secretary General Kofi Annan's call in his 2001 Conflict Prevention Report for "NGOs with an interest in conflict prevention to organise an international conference of local, national and international NGOs on their role in conflict prevention and future interaction with the United Nations in this field." Peace Boat also became the Regional Secretariat for GPPAC in North-East Asia, a role we continue to this day. Through making the most effective use of the expansive human networks nurtured through our Global Voyages, we have been able to make contributions towards promoting GPPAC objectives for conflict prevention and peacebuilding activities.

In 2005, the GPPAC Global Conference was held at the United Nations headquarters in New York. Over 2000 conflict prevention and peacebuilding specialists, NGO activists and representatives of international organisations and governments gathered at this meeting, taking part in concrete discussions on a wide range of themes including peace constitutions and nuclear abolition. At its conclusion, the GPPAC Global Agenda was adopted, in which the concept of 'countries without armies' – as upheld in the Constitutions of Japan and Costa Rica, for example – were recognised as effective mechanisms for conflict prevention, such as playing "an important role in promoting regional stability and increasing confidence." The same document recognised that Article 9 of the Japanese Constitution – which renounces war as a means of settling disputes and maintaining forces for those purposes – "has been a foundation for collective security throughout the Asia-Pacific region."

Following this, Peace Boat has continued to work within the GPPAC framework, collaborating with NGOs throughout the Northeast Asian region to undertake sustained activities advocating a new, peaceful form of regional security. A particular focus of these efforts has been collaboration with Korean NGOs to hold regional conferences engaging both South and North Korea and activities for the denuclearisation of the Korean Peninsula, including joint coordination of a series of critically important 'Civil Society Six-Party Talks'.

'Historical Recognition and History Education' are also a significant focus of Peace Boat's reconciliation activities. For example, Peace Boat has participated in the process of trilateral dialogue in this field between Japanese, Chinese and Korean organisations, as well as utilising our networks throughout Europe to build cooperation between Asian academics and activists creating trilateral joint history textbooks, most notably with Germany's Georg Eckert Institute for International Textbook Research.

Global Article 9 Campaign to Abolish War

A further concrete product of Peace Boat's involvement in the GPPAC network is the Global Article 9 Campaign to Abolish War, mentioned earlier in this book in chapter 8. Article 9 of the Japanese Constitution renounces war as a means of settling international disputes and prohibits the maintenance of armed forces and other war potential. Yet the Japanese government has been moving towards amending Article 9, partly due to the US demand for fully-fledged military support from Japan in its 'war on terror'. Despite the restrictions of Article 9, Japan's Self-Defense Forces have gradually expanded over the past few years, bringing Japan's military expenditure to one of the highest in the world.

In 2005, Peace Boat, together with the Japan Lawyers' International Solidarity Association (JALISA), launched the Global Article 9 Campaign to Abolish War. This campaign strives not only to protect Article 9 locally, but also to build an international movement supporting Article 9 as the shared property of the world, calling for a global peace that does not rely on force.

Indeed, Article 9 is not just a provision of the Japanese law; it also acts as an international peace mechanism towards reductions in military spending, promotion of nuclear-weapon-free zones, ending violence against women, supporting conflict prevention, and mitigating the negative environmental impacts of military processes. International civil society organisations have recognised the global impact of Article 9, including its relevance in regards to human rights, disarmament, nuclear weapons abolition, conflict prevention, development, the environment, globalisation, UN reform and other global issues. Through this campaign, a strong international network has formed, from members of the anti-war movements in the US and elsewhere; to organizations working for peace in Africa or the Middle East; NGOs lobbying for disarmament in Europe; and women's groups acting worldwide.

As a major part of this campaign, the large scale 'Global Article 9 Conference to Abolish War' was held in Japan from 4–6 May 2008. With the participation of Nobel Peace Laureates, intellectuals, cultural figures and NGO activists from over forty countries, this historic three-day conference attracted over 33,000 participants nationwide to join dialogue on the role that citizens of the world can play to realise the principles of Article 9, through promoting disarmament, demilitarisation and a culture of peace.

In a world where the chain of violence and war continues unbroken and militarisation is gathering speed, the existence of Japan's Article 9 provides encouragement to those who work towards a peace that does not rely on force. Article 9 gives hope – hope that another world is possible. The Article 9 Campaign demonstrates the active value of Article 9 and proposes ways to realise its potential.

Global Voyage for a Nuclear-Free World: Peace Boat Hibakusha Project

A great milestone for Peace Boat 2008 was marking the project's twenty-fifth anniversary. As well as hosting the Global Article 9 Conference to

Abolish War, Peace Boat also undertook another new project to share the importance of nonviolence with both its participants on board and people encountered throughout the global journeys.

On the sixty-third Global Voyage for Peace, 103 *Hibakusha* (Atomic Bomb Survivors) of Hiroshima and Nagasaki were invited to join the four-month global journey to share their testimonies of the experience of the atomic bomb with people around the world. Taking place between 7 September 2008 and 13 January 2009, the group visited a total of twenty-three ports in twenty countries, connecting Hibakusha with citizens, NGOs and youth throughout the world, and hoping to add a new breath of life to the global network of citizens working for peace and nuclear abolition.

This project presents an opportunity to reconsider the realities of nuclear weapons together with people from many countries, and to build a foundation of global civil society action towards the abolition of nuclear weapons. The universal message of nuclear disarmament in the voices of Hibakusha was offered to the world. Yet their voices remain marginalised, and the time remaining to hear directly from the Hibakusha is sadly becoming more and more limited.

This historic voyage provided a unique chance to pass along the stories and memories of the Hibakusha, their sufferings and hopes for a nuclear free future. Through direct interaction with youth, citizens, NGOs and victims of wars from other parts of the world, the 103 Hibakusha (from Japan, Korea, Australia, Brazil, Canada and Mexico) acted not only as peace and disarmament educators in raising awareness on the dangers of nuclear weapons and the human costs of war, but also loudly added their voices to the call to abolish all nuclear weapons and create an alternative vision for peace and global stability that does not rely on force or deterrence.

In addition to filming a documentary of the Hibakushas' testimonies and experiences on board (currently in production), public events were held in all ports visited around the world, and interactive programs with local civil society organisations and governmental disarmament officials were organised. For example, during the ship's visit to Sydney in December 2008, the Hibakusha met with local students, Indigenous

Australians victimised by uranium mining, anti-nuclear and environmental activists, politicians and members of the public. They also presented a letter to a representative of Prime Minister Kevin Rudd, in regards to the Australia-Japan initiated International Commission on Nuclear Non-Proliferation and Disarmament (ICNND) established in 2008.

Other activities included a visit by a delegation of Hibakusha to the United Nations headquarters in New York where they gave a presentation to the First Committee at the UN General Assembly's sixty-third session, and the Hibakusha's call succeeding in twenty-seven cities in four countries (Eritrea, Turkey, Spain, Venezuela) joining the Mayors for Peace Initiative.

Furthermore, the Hibakusha were able to strengthen solidarity with other nuclear victims and war survivors throughout the world, including victims of nuclear testing in Tahiti and uranium mining in Australia. The voyage also acted to revitalise the Hibakusha movement itself. Amongst the participants were Hibakusha who had never before told their stories to others, let alone in public, who shared their experiences for the first time. 'Young Hibakusha', infants or young children in 1945, who have no direct recollection of the atomic bombing were also involved. Furthermore, the project featured great collaboration between youth and Hibakusha, both amongst the 700 participants on board the Peace Boat itself, and also within the places visited around the world. The second Peace Boat Hibakusha Project will be held on board the sixty-seventh Global Voyage, taking place from 8 August–22 November 2009.

Sailing on: the future of Peace Boat

Peace Boat's strength is in the special potential of its unique space: floating at sea and transcending borders, it brings people away from the pressures of their everyday lives and at the same time to a point where they can see the complexity and humanity of our world in sharp relief. That is, they see peace in all its dimensions – economic, social, political and environmental – and understand that this view of promoting peace with justice begins with increasing our literacy about nonviolence as the key to a thriving humanity.

In this era in which our world appears to be getting ever smaller, with the Internet and Skype communications making contact with people from across the planet easier and cheaper, there is less reliance on meeting people face-to-face or being able to grasp their hand whilst sharing experiences. It is this kind of contact that enables the growth of deep solidarity. As the threats posed by environmental degradation and climate change begin to have an increasingly severe impact on the lives of people in many parts of the world, it will be essential to understand the grassroots effect of our choices on other people's lives.

As the *New York Times* famously wrote on the occasion of the February 2003 Anti-Iraqi War demonstrations, "there may still be two superpowers on the planet: the United States and world public opinion." Four years later, I was in the offices of the European Union in Brussels and a top-level official confided in me, whilst speaking of Baghdad, that "the world's largest army cannot even keep order in a medium-sized city". Traditional means of organising the world order are no longer acceptable, or even feasible. This century is the century of global civil society.

Peace Boat has a significant part to play in this developing global society and must continue to expand its role in bringing people together and supporting global citizenship. In fact, I have a dream … of being able to open up the ship in a manner that will truly go beyond borders: political borders, social borders, economic borders, and corporate borders. I dream of a 'Peace Boat Passport', through which we guarantee and protect the work of our nonviolence practitioners and, in our shared solidarity, are able to work in equality and without encumbrances across the borders of nationality. The Peace Boat project is a single example and a relatively small-scale project, with ambitious goals and significant challenges in thinking about regional and global governance, the limits of nation states, and our duty as citizens of the world to struggle together for a peaceful and sustainable planet.

AFTERWORD

Learning and doing: the genesis of CPACS

Mary Lane

6 March 1985: a large, airy classroom in the Mills Building, Sydney University. Seventeen fourth-year social work students are filing in, chatting animatedly, keen to get going in this final year of their social work degree – four men, thirteen women, and a mix of mature-aged and younger students.[1] *I am already in the room, perched beside a table with a pile of information about the Community Work course upon which we are about to embark. I am welcoming the students, none of whom I have met before. My greetings perhaps reveal a touch of apprehension as I am planning a learning experience quite different to that usually associated with universities.*

We begin ... and unbeknown to us then, so does the story of CPACS.

> Just as no man lives or dies to himself, so no experience lives and dies to itself. Wholly independent of desire or intent, every experience lives on in further experiences. Hence the central problem of an education based upon experience is to select the kind of present experiences that live fruitfully and creatively in subsequent experience (Dewey 1963, pp. 27–28).

---

1 Vince Beer, Annette Clynes, Janet Donnelly, Louise Finnegan, Andrew Gavrielatis, Alix Goodwin, Sandy Gowing, Peter Hampson, Kristen Henderson, Kaylene Henry, Claire Hogan, Kate Johnson, Cathy Newman, Ric Norton, Jenny Ow, Maria Trevato and Amanda Watts.

The Community Work class, an option in the fourth year, undergraduate Social Work Practice 2 course, drew on the principles of experiential, dialogical and participatory education. I had long been attracted to John Dewey's ideas about experiential learning, and Paola Freire's dialogical, participatory approaches (Dewey 1963; Freire 1972, 1974). These had significantly influenced my previous community work practice and teaching. The option however, was the first time I endeavoured to fully embrace 'learning through doing' in a university-based course. I wanted the students to learn about community work by actually doing it. Involvement in a 'real life' project would be the means for gaining skills, knowledge and conceptual understandings about community work – a means for linking theories and practices. Something on campus should be manageable, I thought. The course handout described what I had in mind:

> The class will firstly pick an issue which is identified as a problem, need or interest of the student 'community'. The group will then proceed to take action on this issue to achieve their ends (Community Work Option 1985, Social Work Practice II 1985).

The open-ended nature of experiential learning created an edge of anxiety for all of us. So did the challenge of doing a group project which students realised would be demanding of time and effort. Nevertheless, they were excited by the idea of a course with a difference and we set off with enthusiasm towards our unknown destination.

Initially, I was uncertain about how far I should adhere to dialogical experiential learning, knowing that students were far more familiar with teacher-directed, didactic approaches. I, too, found it hard to let go of the idea that there was a body of explanatory theories and practice strategies which I should impart to students, particularly at the beginning of the option, as background to their future thoughts and actions. Would project happenings provide enough opportunities for me to weave in such material along the way?

I took a cautious approach, easing us into experiential learning by allocating time in the first three sessions for 'conventional' teaching about community work concepts, theories and strategies (lecture/

overhead format), as well as time for project discussion. I soon found though, that I could link material I was introducing with the class discussions about a project, which at this stage was about finding an issue. For example, using each of their project suggestions, I asked them to consider: the aims, values and political ideologies behind their proposals; who or what they saw as 'community'; how the need or issue they suggested had been identified and by whom; what community work strategies might be involved and what they were most interested in – social action, service development, advocacy … ?

These early sessions thus helped me to see how I could match my input with project happenings. From then on, I was able to put aside the idea that I should provide blocks of information separated from lived experience. I became more adept at weaving in community work theories and practices as situations arose, encouraging discussion and analysis and drawing attention to appropriate readings as we went.

Looking at the way we learned is one of the stories to be told about the class of '85. It is a way consistent with community development processes and values whereby participation and equality amongst group members is nurtured through emphasis on consensus decision making and the sharing of tasks and roles. The focus of the story I tell here is, however, not about analysing the educational process itself; it's more about describing happenings, that is, what we did and how this led to the birth of CPACS.

Our doings can be seen as a classic piece of social action characterised by several identifiable stages. I note though, that whilst emphasis was on particular tasks at particular times, stages and tasks overlapped and events were sometimes cyclical. Goals were continually being refined, actions evaluated, and resources sought – information, people and material resources. Further, the crucial issue of group maintenance defies description through a 'stages' approach. As with all sustainable groups, ensuring positive group dynamics was an ongoing task always needing attention. My role was one of the questions the group had to address throughout, as was the need to maximise inclusion and to work out ways of sharing tasks and information. Later, we struggled with tensions between informal/formal ways of running the group, and dealt with frustrations about the length of time tasks were taking. All these issues were typical of those which arise in community groups at any, and often all, stages of action.

Nevertheless, analysis of the comprehensive records kept from day one[2] reveals an unfolding of events which lends itself to description through reference to certain stages and tasks typically associated with community action: identifying an issue; informing ourselves about that issue; contacting people to assess interest and identify allies; maintaining the group; bringing people together to form an action group; building resources and broadening support; refining strategies; achieving goals.

Identifying an issue

In the first few weeks the dominant task was finding a project issue. By the third week, student suggestions had boiled down to three: tertiary education fees, racism on campus, and peace – the latter as yet perceived very generally apart from one suggestion about seeking a nuclear-free university. One of the students supporting peace came well prepared, arguing that this would be particularly appropriate as it was International Youth Year and the themes for the year were participation, development and peace. Her opinions seemed to carry a lot of weight in the group.

In a more detailed account, I have described the process of issue selection (Lane, forthcoming). I quote from that part of the account which refers to the final moments of the process, as we can now see that this was a crucial time in the history of CPACS. The room is tense, class time is running out and people are weary after a lengthy session trying to reach consensus:

> It was proving very hard to make a decision. We needed five or ten minutes more, but session time was running out. No one wanted to force a decision. Someone said, "let's have a vote", and there were exhausted nods all round. One of the group members offered to write the suggestions on the board

---

2 As well as detailed handwritten notes I scribbled during, after and before each class, records include minutes of meetings, press releases, letters, and fliers about events. Many of these records are archived in the CPACS library, Sydney University.

and as no one disagreed she got up to do that. It changed the dynamics of the meeting as I then sat in her chair and she became a sort of leader, standing out front, directing the vote. There were none for tertiary fees, nine for peace, when someone queried, "is Mary voting?" I asked them whether they wanted me to, as I hadn't intended to do so. There was agreement that I should and I made a vote for peace (perhaps sitting within the group was a levelling experience and they now saw me more as one of them). Seven then voted for the racism on campus issue.[3]

Voting has winners and losers but the group accepted the decision, being relieved, I think, to have at last made a start on finding an issue. I tried to lessen any fall out by pointing out that anti-racism and peace were closely connected; we might find we could deal with racism within the peace issue. For the moment, we needed to inform ourselves about 'peace' and come up with a more specific focus for our project. Our peace research began.

Informing ourselves

I was pleased the group chose peace. Before the vote I had concealed my preference, knowing that if they were to own the project and maintain enough enthusiasm to carry it through, they would have to choose it themselves. Fortuitously though, peace was also an issue of much interest to me; I had been involved in the peace movement since the Vietnam War years. Initially, I had associated peace with anti-war activity but over time my understanding had broadened. I owed much to Stella Cornelius for my education about peace and conflict. In the early 1980s, as a member of the National Women's Advisory Council, I managed to get peace on to the Council's agenda (NATWAC Annual Report 1982–83). Whilst helping to organise a seminar on peace for the June 1983 meeting, I contacted Stella and other key figures in the Australian peace movement, including Nancy Shelley, a Canberra

---

3 Sixteen students voted. The class included 17 people in all. My records do not show whether someone was away or someone abstained. Peace would still have narrowly prevailed even if the missing person had voted for racism on campus.

peace activist.⁴ These people introduced me to a breadth of literature and ideas. You can't have sustainable peace without social justice, they argued; the absence of war is not enough. The knowledge I gained gave me confidence that I could resource our class project about peace.

It was a good time to be doing something about peace, a time of much public and government activity around disarmament and anti-nuclear issues. The Federal Labor government, elected in 1983, had taken some important initiatives (Hayden 1983). An Ambassador for Disarmament had been appointed, and the government was supporting the setting up of an independent peace research body at the Australian National University. It was also supporting a comprehensive nuclear test ban treaty and looking at ways to introduce peace studies into schools and tertiary institutions.

Expanding our conceptual understanding of peace and gathering information about peace initiatives, particularly within universities, were major tasks for the group. Apart from one or two students, the group had limited understanding of the conceptual complexity of peace and only vague ideas about what was happening around peace issues on campus.

We began by pooling knowledge and material we already had – literature, an audiotape Stella had given me, and a video brought in by the student who had originally suggested we work on a peace project. The information reflected broad conceptualisations of peace and broad goals for action, such as campaigning for disarmament and a nuclear-free Pacific, and setting up a Ministry of Peace. Significantly for us though, suggestions for action also included those 'closer to home': setting up peace research centres at universities, promoting peace studies, seeking nuclear-free universities, and reducing racial discrimination at universities.

We also tuned into our networks for ideas about specific projects. This had a 'snowballing' effect leading us to people who were pursuing peace

---

4 Stella Cornelius founded the Conflict Resolution Network in Sydney and in 1984–86 was Director of the Australian Government's Secretariat for United Nations International Year of Peace; Nancy Shelley, a peace activist living in Canberra, was active on many peace fronts including WILPF – Women's International League for Peace and Freedom.

initiatives at universities.[5] We found, for example, that there was a peace studies course at Macquarie University in Sydney, and further afield a university which had set up a thriving Peace Studies Department and a comprehensive peace library – Bradford University in England. We couldn't find any courses specifically labelled as such on our campus but we started to uncover some interest in peace issues, including within our own department.[6]

In some ways our initial information gathering made it harder to find a specific focus for a peace project. There were so many possibilities. Time for decision making was proving a problem for us too. Two visits to the field in these early weeks broadened student knowledge about community work practice but limited time for project discussion. By the seventh week frustrations were running high. To this point, I had adopted non-directive roles trying to encourage students to find their own way, but I now decided to push things along – using my change of style as a topic for discussion about directiveness and non-directiveness in community work. I listed all the project possibilities students had suggested, the most favoured of which were peace studies, a nuclear free University, and racism on campus, and I bluntly pointed out: "We can't do it all. What's the issue? What are our aims?"

A few students wanted to further explore the meaning of peace before making a decision. The majority argued, "let's get on with it" (the words of one of the more task-oriented students). That approach prevailed, and by the end of the session the group had chosen a priority. We would seek the introduction of peace studies at Sydney University.

With renewed energy we went into task mode to gather more information about peace studies courses at universities, identify people who might lend support, and explore possible funding sources. Six of us visited Gary Simpson who co-ordinated the course at Macquarie University. Gary was located in Education but many Schools were involved in the

---

5 These included: Sabina Erica and Gary Simpson at Macquarie University, NSW; Ralph Summy, Griffith University, Queensland; Tony Kelly, Brenda Lewis and Ros Mills, Queensland University; and Keith Suter, Wesley College, Sydney University.

6 For example, a colleague, Alec Pemberton ran a sociology course on war and peace. Another, Alan Davis, had links with SANA – Scientists Against Nuclear Arms.

teaching and supplying of students. He emphasised the importance of a multidisciplinary approach, argued for a social justice viewpoint, and advised against nuclear sensationalism and a statistical perspective. He told us that evaluation highlighted their course should be more feminist-oriented and include more on environmental issues. Gary's ideas gave weight to the values and directions towards which we'd been leaning. From that meeting too, we realised that an important question for us would be the location of courses. At Sydney there wasn't the flexibility between Faculties that Macquarie had between its Schools.

New challenges arose when we sought a small grant from International Youth Year to assist our activities and start building a peace library. We were not a constituted body so we needed a sponsor. The Social Work Student Association agreed to do this, but who were we? Poring over the submission, the discussion went like this:

"We'll have to have a name." Momentary silence. Then, quick as a flash, Ric piped up, "SCIPS – Student Committee for the Introduction of Peace Studies." Laughs and yeses all round. Great Ric!

SCIPS was launched!

It was 22 April, a day that we also refined our tactics. We would find out more about what was happening in different Departments at Sydney University and see if interested staff would come to a meeting in second term to discuss campaigning for peace studies. It was a tangible goal to work towards.

Contacting, contacting and more contacting ...

By the end of first term, extensive contacting had revealed considerable interest in the teaching of peace and conflict studies on our campus. In community work language the class was building a 'community profile' of what was happening, and what might be possible. Interest was multidisciplinary, supportive people being identified in a range of Departments including Government, Education, History, Medicine, Social Work and Sociology, Political Economy, Chemistry, and Law. Some were already teaching courses related to peace. The notion of a separate centre for peace studies within the University was raised by at least two of the people contacted. All in all, the students found that interest in peace was more prevalent amongst academics than they had thought; the problem had been a lack of publicity about what people were doing and no identified network. There was now much support for the idea of a meeting to bring interested people together.

It was a good note on which to end the term. There was a feeling of promise that we were involved in a movement which would not be stopped.

Maintaining ourselves

Group maintenance was ongoing, but there were several points in our project when it became an urgent issue requiring special attention if we were to move on effectively. Throughout the project we endeavoured to work in participatory ways which would nurture group cohesion and individual satisfaction. Efforts to promote participation and consensus were, however, sometimes in tension with getting tasks done, particularly when there were time pressures. Frustrations would emerge requiring us to review our way of operating. Such had been the case when we resorted to a vote when choosing peace for a project. A more serious challenge to group cohesion arose when we met in early June after the term break. I recount what happened as project outcomes might well have been different if we had not resolved this and other group tensions along the way.

We were at a crucial stage of the project and the way forward was clearer, though somewhat daunting, the meeting with interested staff needing to be held before the end of July when the Option finished. But there were other reasons contributing to the student frustrations which now burst out:

"We're not getting anywhere"; "I feel alienated, some are doing all the work"; "when you miss a meeting you don't know what's going on – the telephone tree isn't working"; "there's too much chaos"; "we want more fun".

When I asked what we needed to do,[7] they were just as forthcoming:

---

[7] For educators adopting experiential learning approaches, as for community workers adopting enabling roles, there is a delicate balance between using one's own experience to suggest ways of doing things, and letting people come to their

"Group efficiency needs looking at"; "we need clearer roles for people"; "we need to plan our time better".

A more formal group structure was worked out, one which sought to increase both participation and efficiency. This included identifying a convenor and minute taker for each session (both tasks to be rotated weekly; the convenor responsible for drawing up an agenda), and arranging a more efficient system for distributing minutes and other information.

Opting for more structure was an interesting turn of events – and a common one in groups when time is limited and the need to get tasks done calls for emphasis on increased efficiency. We were under pressure. We had floated an issue, raised expectations and set a date for the meeting, 2 July. We had just four weeks to organise it.

Bringing people together around a common interest

In preparing for the meeting we continued to inform ourselves about the conceptual complexities of peace, gather further information about what was happening at universities around Australia, and seek advice about the best ways of getting peace studies going at Sydney University.[8] A key contact at this stage was Keith Suter, whom we invited to a class session. Keith was based at Wesley College, Sydney University, and was well known, nationally and internationally, for his work in peace and conflict.[9] His view was to aim for a peace with justice perspective and to have "a smorgasbord of content" – a perspective further reinforcing the directions we had been developing.

Keith told us about earlier efforts at Sydney University to introduce

---

own conclusions from their *own* experiences. In this case I emphasised the latter course, even though I was somewhat unsure, not wishing to model an ineffective community work style. Confidence in the learning approach and a healthy ego is required!

8 Information we obtained included a very useful summary of peace studies courses at Australian Universities, produced by the Victorian Association of Peace Studies, circa 1984.

9 Keith Suter later became involved with the Centre for Peace and Conflict Studies (CPACS) and was President of CPACS, 1991–1996.

peace studies, including those of Peter King in the Department of Government. Peter was coming to our July meeting and had assured us of his support. We were alerted to finding out more about these previous attempts.[10]

Another crucial meeting task was to clarify our aims and hoped-for outcomes. We sought a sharing of information about what we and others were already doing about peace studies at Sydney University and elsewhere; and we sought to look at ways in which the work on our campus might be extended. If the movement was to continue, we needed to ensure follow up from the meeting. We were all too aware that the Community Work Option would finish soon and the students would leave campus for their final fieldwork placement. Would any remain involved? This created a feeling of panic in me particularly! To whom would the mantle be passed? One idea floated in class discussions was to try and come away from the 2 July meeting with a staff/student working party.

The meeting day arrived, 2 July 1985. We were quietly confident, extensive contacting having confirmed considerable staff interest in our purposes. But we were also apprehensive, wondering whether interest would translate into action to carry the movement forward. We had prepared well for this moment but much was at stake.

All seventeen students in the SCIPS group and ten academics were present.[11] Information sharing revealed initiatives already happening: courses on war and peace in the Departments of Social Work and of History; a course on the consequences of ionising radiation run by the Institute of Molecular Biology; and a $60,000 International Year of Peace (IYP) grant received by Charles Kerr to research people's thinking about nuclear war. Next year (1986, IYP year), the Asian Peace Research

---

10 Peter King became a key player in the movement to set up CPACS, and was its first President, 1988–1990.

11 In addition to myself, staff at the July 2 meeting were: Alec Pemberton and Christian Alexander (Social Work), Charles Kerr (Public Health and Tropical Medicine), Peter King (Government), Gavan Butler (Economics), John Burnheim (General Philosophy), Chris Dos Remedios (Anatomy), Bob Hunter (Chemistry), and Peter Castaldi (Medicine). Enrico Petazzoni from Economics sent an apology.

Conference would be held at Sydney University, and the Department of Government was planning a peace studies course.

The educational value of an interdisciplinary approach was emphasised. Whilst organisational difficulties were foreseen with inter-faculty courses, ongoing contact between staff teaching peace-related courses in different Departments was seen as important, as was the notion of setting up a working party to establish an interdisciplinary Peace Research Centre which would offer postgraduate research opportunities. A further suggestion, one more easily attainable in the short term, was to run lunchtime seminars on peace issues. SCIPS was delegated the task of drawing up an agenda for future action and calling another meeting.

It was a very positive response to our meeting purposes. Soon afterwards, our efforts were further heartened when the research officer in the Department of Social Work, Annette Hay, offered to collect information for us and build up a research file on peace issues – the beginnings, as we saw it, of a resource centre. She had already gathered some readings including some from Great Britain forcefully arguing against peace studies – a perspective we needed to consider, and counter, when presenting our arguments for peace studies at Sydney University.[12]

Hanging over these positive outcomes, though, was the spectre of time. The Community Work class was due to end 31 July. It was urgent that we now focus on the question of who would be left to 'carry the baby'. Some of the SCIPS group needed to move on; others, including myself, were committed to carrying on the project but our numbers would be small, just six or so of us. If we were to maintain a strong student component in the movement, as we wanted, we needed to direct our efforts to seeking their involvement. To this end, the final weeks of class saw us organising meetings with second and third year Social Work students. A handful of third years responded[13] and joined up with SCIPS

---

12 Annette Hay uncovered for us a vigorous debate in Britain (reported in *The Times*, 1984), between those supporting and those opposing peace studies in schools and universities. Vocal critics were Caroline Cox and Roger Scruton, authors of *Peace studies: a critical survey*, published in London by the Institute for European Defence and Strategic Studies, 1984.

13 Two third year students, Joe Rosa and Penny May, went on to make a significant contribution to the work which culminated in the setting up of CPACS in 1988.

people to continue the outreach to students and prepare for the follow up meeting with staff. The future of SCIPS itself in events to come was unclear but all were agreed that decisions about its future should be made by the continuing members.

We said our farewells. It had been a challenging course, with huge commitment from this small bunch of students. For some it was now over. For others, it was just the completion of the first chapter of the SCIPS story.

Building resources, broadening support: from SCIPS to SSCIPS

The immediate focus for the now smaller SCIPS group was the second meeting with staff, set for 13 September.[14] Our main aim was to encourage the emergence of a working party of students and staff that would follow up ideas flagged in the initial meeting. Again, we prepared well, gathering further information about initiatives at Australian universities to set up peace research centres and organise seminars on peace.[15]

A small but enthusiastic group of staff turned up to the meeting. The multidisciplinary aspect, which SCIPS had worked so hard to achieve, was reinforced; staff attending came from Social Work, Chemistry, Economics, Government, and Medicine.[16] A working party of staff and students began work immediately, organising a series of four lunchtime seminars about the arms race to be held in October.

---

14 The seven students now in the SCIPS group were: Louise Finnegan, Alix Goodwin, Sandy Gowing, Kaylene Henry, and Ric Norton from the community work class; Penny May and Jo Rosa from third year social work.

15 Initiatives at Australian universities included the Peace Research Centre at the Australian National University; and lunchtime seminars at Newcastle and Monash Universities.

16 Present at the meeting were: Bob Hunter (Chemistry), Enrico Petazzoni (Economics), Peter King (Government), Susan Ballinger (Medicine), Annette Hay and Mary Lane (Social Work). Charles Kerr (Public Health and Tropical Medicine) sent an apology. The network of support for SSCIPS now also included people from Education, History, Law, and Philosophy. Soon after this September meeting it further expanded to include people from Pharmacy, Physics, Pure Mathematics, Botany, Engineering, Wesley College and Fisher Library.

We were now SSCIPS – Staff/Student Committee for the Introduction of Peace Studies. Student involvement remained influential, with social work students (including several from the original SCIPS group) taking on the roles of convenor and minute taker, as well as being involved in organising other activities.

Lunchtime seminars soon became a regular feature of SSCIPS work. They were a particularly useful means for catching the interest of students and staff and spreading the word about SSCIPS's ultimate goals – the promotion of peace studies and the establishment of a Peace Centre. Achieving these long-term goals received a boost when Roger Wescombe, at that time Deputy Director of International House at the University, joined SSCIPS and organised a Peace Studies Workshop in June 1986 to explore strategies. Forty-five people attended, and staff from a range of Departments spoke about the possibilities of introducing peace studies into their courses. The culmination of the workshop was agreement through a formal motion that a Peace Centre be established at Sydney University (Interim Council CPACS minutes, 25 February 1988). I remember well the euphoria I felt at that moment.

With in-principle support from a wide range of disciplines, focus for SSCIPS was now on the detail of establishing a Centre. Obtaining the agreement of the Vice-Chancellor and drawing up a constitution were key tasks. Being aware of possible opposition from the University hierarchy to the study of peace, we changed the name of the centre being sought to the Centre for Peace and Conflict Studies – conflict, it seemed, having more credibility in academia! (SSCIPS minutes, 11 September 1986).

It was almost two more years though, before the long-term goal of a Centre was realised. A constitution which would reflect SSCIPS's values of participatory democracy at the same time as being acceptable to the University administration took months to negotiate. Letters from SSCIPS to the Vice Chancellor's office went unanswered for weeks, and things dragged on. It seemed the Vice Chancellor and other hierarchy were unconvinced about the academic credibility of peace studies;[17]

---

17 A letter dated 19 January 1988, from the Vice Chancellor to SSCIPS member Dr Peter King indicates this was the case. Referring to papers concerning the

perhaps SSCIPS was not forceful or smart enough in its advocacy. Whatever the reason, little was happening in terms of gaining the Vice Chancellor's approval for a Centre and our energy was being sapped by frustration. It was as well that our hopes were kept alive by committed staff and students, the success of the lunchtime seminars, and a visit in May 1987 from world renowned peace scholars, Elise and Kenneth Boulding.

Refining strategies, achieving goals

It was clear we needed to rethink our strategy and seek more effective ways of achieving our primary goal. Someone who might help was 'under our noses' – Stuart Rees, Professor of Social Work and Head of Department. The Department had been supportive of the movement since its very beginnings, supplying the venue for the group's meetings, housing the resource library, and absorbing many of the day-by-day administrative costs. Most recently, the Department had been approached with a request from SSCIPS for space to locate a Centre. Social work students had always been at the heart of the cause and continued to play vital roles, contributing especially to administrative tasks, organising seminars and building support for a Centre. Social Work staff were also prominent players. Roger Wescombe (now in the Department as the Administration Officer),[18] and myself were members of SSCIPS; others, whilst not directly involved, had followed the movement with keen interest, lending advice and support when called upon. One of these was Stuart. Politically 'savvy' and a member of the University governing body, the Senate, he had access to the top echelons of the University. Now was the time to seek his more direct involvement.

---

proposed Centre for Peace and Conflict Studies, sent to the VC by Dr King in March 1987, the letter reads: "I have had problems with some of the academic aspects of the proposal and have considered them with the advice of some of our colleagues". The VC goes on to suggest Dr King gets in touch again to discuss the problems.

18 Roger Wescombe's understanding of the University bureaucracy was particularly valuable in organisational issues such as drawing up a constitution for CPACS.

It was late 1987. I knew Stuart was overstretched for time, but determination to gain a Centre gave me confidence to put the question. I found the appropriate moment in the early morning quietness of the photocopying room before the Department erupted into busyness – a mundane context for what was to be an important conversation for the future of CPACS: "We're not getting anywhere fast with the Centre, we need your assistance; we're setting up an Interim Council until the constitution's formalised and we want you on it; you could push things along – it would be great if you'd come to SSCIPS meetings". He did so and was there at the next meeting in December.

Stuart's proactive involvement from that time on was to prove the boost we needed. He agreed to convene a small group to get things moving. Together with long-time SSCIPS members, Peter King and Bob Hunter, and SSCIPS convenor Igor Gonda, he wrote to the Vice Chancellor in early February 1988 putting the case for a Centre and requesting a meeting. There were strong arguments including broad interdisciplinary support from within and outside the University, promise of a location in the Mills Building, and precedents for such centres in several prestigious universities in North America, Britain and Scandinavia. Adding further credibility to the group's efforts was the arrival of the first visiting scholar, Dr. Gordon Rodley, a New Zealand specialist on deterrence and disarmament.

It was a well-organised group of about ten SSCIPS supporters that eventually met with the Vice Chancellor on 28 March 1988. It seems our efforts had already been successful, and needing no further convincing the Vice Chancellor agreed with the setting up of the Centre. After three years of trying, it was an unexpectedly easy meeting – a denouement par excellence!

And so ... to CPACS

The rest is well-known history: the announcement by the Vice Chancellor to the Senate on 5 April that a Centre for Peace and Conflict Studies had been established in the University; the launch of the Centre on 16 May by the then Minister of Defence, Kim Beazley; the winding up of SSCIPS, its work now done, at the first Annual General meeting of the Centre on 14 July; and the struggles of the infant CPACS to survive with few resources and tensions within the organisation over priorities and ways of going about things (Rees 1990, pp. 19–25).

There was, however, a firm foundation upon which to build the organisation. The legacy bequeathed to CPACS was more than a group of people committed to seeing it flourish; it was to do with certain values and principles which guided the work of the original student group (SCIPS) and then the staff/student group (SSCIPS). I mention here just three influential aspects. Firstly, the peace with justice perspective. Adopted initially by the student group, it survived the challenges posed when SCIPS expanded to include staff from many disciplines and diverse theoretical backgrounds. It was then that differences emerged as to where the emphasis of peace work should lie. For some, emphasis was on the study of war, nuclear disarmament and deterrence; others favoured emphasis on the structural and cultural aspects of peace and violence, such as tackling poverty, promoting democracy and building civil society. Differences of emphasis sometimes led to tensions but there remained general agreement that the pursuit of sustainable peace entailed a peace with justice perspective and a broad understanding of factors associated with peace and conflict. It was a perspective carried over to the fledgling CPACS.

Hand in hand with this conceptualisation of peace went the notions of interdisciplinarity and multidisciplinarity. From the very beginnings of the movement, co-operation between people from different, and many, disciplines had provided theoretical and strategic strength. Inter- and multidisciplinarity were well established aspects of the movement, modelling the way for baby CPACS.

A third legacy was evidence of the importance of group maintenance. Early in the movement the student group had identified this as something requiring ongoing attention. Lapses in attending to group maintenance occurred later in the staff/student group (SSCIPS) when differences arose about priorities, and tensions were exacerbated by the frustrations of a drawn out campaign. The message for CPACS was that both SCIPS and SSCIPS worked most effectively and happily when they did so in ways consistent with the Gandhian notion of 'peace is the way'. It was an understanding which nurtured maximum participation, consensus decision making, sharing of responsibilities, open flow of information, and airing and negotiation of differences through fair process.

Reference to the old cliché, 'from little things big things grow' may seem corny but it fits the story of CPACS. Achievements over the last 20 years have been impressive, among them the spawning of the Sydney Peace Foundation and CPACS's growth as a nationally and internationally respected teaching and research centre. It's a great story and it's remarkable to think that it all started with a small bunch of students in the Class of '85. We did John Dewey (1963, pp. 27–28) proud:

> Just as no man lives or dies to himself, so no experience lives and dies to itself. Wholly independent of desire or intent, every experience lives on in further experiences.

This volume is testament to the ongoing work of CPACS in thinking about war and crafting peace.

References

Commonwealth of Australia (1984). *National Women's Advisory Council, Annual Report 1982–83*. Canberra: Australian Government Publishing Service, p. 22.

Dewey, J. (1963). *Experience and education*. New York: Collier.

Freire, P. (1972). *Pedagogy of the oppressed*. Harmondsworth, London: Penguin Books.

Freire, P. (1974). *Education for critical consciousness*. London: Sheed and Ward.

Hayden, B. (1983). *1983 H.V. Evatt Memorial Lecture*. Adelaide, 7 July.

Interim Council of the Centre for Peace and Conflict Studies (1988). Minutes of Inaugural Meeting, 25 February. CPACS archives.

Lane, M. (forthcoming). Work in progress on a book about community work in NSW.

Rees, S. (1990). The politics of peace and conflict studies: social work skills affecting organisations' processes, priorities and project outcomes. *Australian Social Work,* 43(2): 19–25.

Staff/Student Committee for the Introduction of Peace Studies (1986). Minutes of meeting 11 September1986. CPACS archives.

The University of Sydney, Department of Social Work (1985). Community Work Option 1985, Social Work Practice II. Private collection.

INDEX

A
Abu Ghraib xv, 75
Aboriginal people 128, *see also* Indigenous people
  and land 123
activism
  anti-Iraq demonstrations 162
  anti-war movement 123, 159, 167
  human shield vii, 5, 39, 144
  peace protests 95, 127, 137–49, 151–60
Afghanistan x, 5, 39, 41, 71–76, 101, 106, 113, 118–19, 121, 143, 157
Africa, ix, 34, 96, 115–16, 121, 153–54, 159
Al-Jazeera 76, 72
Al-Qaeda 71–72
Amnesty
  International, 25, 29, 52
  Law, 116, 119
Annan, Kofi 114, 157
anti-ballistic missile, 125
Arafat, Yasser 73

Australian Anti-Bases Campaign Coalition x, 123–33
axis of evil 65

B
bin Laden, Osama 74, 115
Blair, Tony xiv, xv, 65, 77
Brecht, Bertolt 15
Britain, xiii–xiv, 26–27, 65, 92, 95, 99, 122, 138, 140, 152, 174, 178 *see also* Blair, Tony
Bush, George W. xiv, 4, 12, 65, 67, 77, 78, 95, 98, 106, 157
  administration xiv, 12, 65, 157

C
capitalism 6, 103, 108, 153
  'disaster' vi, 104, 110
Centre for Peace and Conflict Studies v, viii–xi, 27, 163–80
citizenship
  global/international 162, 159
civil liberties xi, xviii, 74–75, 79
civil society x, 7, 73–74, 151, 156, 159–60, 162, 179

clash of civilisations 20, 45, 65, 138
climate change 19, 26, 162
coalition of the willing 4, 66, 70
Cold War vii, ix, 152, 153, 156
conflict 33, 154–55, 157, 159, 167, 170, 172, 176, 179–80
Conflict Resolution Network vii, 168
Cornelius, Stella vii, 167, 168
crimes against humanity 38, 115

D

Dallaire, Roméo 113–15, 120
democracy vi, xiv, 8, 11, 19, 24, 28, 63, 75, 144, 153–54, 176, 179
development 33, 107, 131, 153, 159, 166
  community xviii, 165
  aid 46, 104
dialogue vii, xviii, xx, 3, 8, 154–56, 158–59
disarmament 113–19, 159–61, 168, 178 *see also* nuclear disarmament

E

education
  human rights ix, 37, 46, 38
  peace xi, 151, 154, 160 *also see* peace studies
environment x, 38, 40, 42–43, 45–47, 50, 58, 98, 128, 153–54, 159, 170

F

Fallujah vii, 36, 137–38, 141, 143–49, 150
foreign policy xiii, 34, 109
  and international relations 73–74
  Australian 143
  United States' 73–74, 77

G

Galtung, Johan vi
Geneva Convention(s) 27, 138, 140, 149
genocide 26, 30, 49, 55, 100
Global Action to Prevent War (GAPW) xxii
Gulf War 20, 36, 101, 111, 124

H

Hibakusha Project 159–61
Hope, A.D. xvi
Howard, John xiv, xix, 25, 30, 143,
humanitarian(ism) xi
  aid worker xi
human rights xviii, xix, 33, 41, 45, 58, 62, 100, 114, 119, 152, 159
  education ix
  law 100
Hussein, Saddam xiii, xv, xxi, 36, 39, 65, 67, 75, 77, 97–99, 101

I

Indigenous
  peoples, 128, 160

cultures 108
International Commission on Nuclear Non-Proliferation and Disarmament (ICNND) 161
international law xv–xviii, 19, 27–29, 100, 157
humanitarian 100
and protection 13 *see also* Responsibility to Protect
intervention 66, 77, 104, 109, 103
military 71, 138
Iran xiv, xv, 20, 43, 57, 66–71, 75, 78, 96, 123
Iraq v, 20, 21, 24, 30, 43, 47, 56, 65–81, 85, 97, 99–101, 104, 106, 110–11, 113, 115, 117, 119, 121, 123, 132, 143–45, 157
Baghdad xi, xiv, 19, 26, 28, 70, 72, 87, 89–90, 97, 102, 108, 143, 145–47, 162
invasion of vi, 7, 19–20, 26, 49, 66–68, 72, 75, 78
war v, xv, 71–72, 77, 79–80, 123
Israel xviii, 66, 69–71, 74–75, 78, 154–55

J

Japan Constitution
Article 9 118, 120, 158–59
junk politics 8
justice vi, xviii, xx, 117, 152,
achieving 73

and accountability 27
and equality 57
and injustice 3, 107
divine vii, 12–13
juvenile ix
peace with v, vii, xxi, xxii, 113, 115, 116, 118, 119, 120, 153, 155, 161, 172, 179
pursuit of 29, 116
social 45, 168, 170
systems of xx
just peace xiii, xvii, xx, 3, 120
just war 3, 117

K

Kipling, Rudyard 6
Klein, Naomi 104, 108

L

Lebanon xii, 40, 66, 68–70, 73, 75, 79

M

Mayors for Peace Initiative 161
media vi, xv–xvi, 20–24, 26–28, 30, 35–39
Medical Association for the Prevention of War (MAPW) vii, xii
military vi, xviii, 93–94, 96, 98, 108–09, 158–59
military-industrial complex 93, 50, 107
Millennium Development Goals 38

Index **185**

N

national interest 3, 76, 117
neo-liberalism 103, 107, 109
nonviolence iv, vi–vii, xv, xx, 15, 123, 125–29, 151, 154, 160–62
nuclear
　disarmament 92, 159, 160, 161, 168, 179
　non-proliferation 122, 161,
　Non-Proliferation Treaty 94, 161
　weapons 42–45, 92, 159

O

Obama, Barack 19, 66, 71, 78, 100, 105–06, 123
　administration 66, 123
Operation Iraqi Freedom 102, 104
Oxfam 33, 35, 36, 50

P

pacifism/pacifist iv, xvi, 3
Palestine xi, 74–75, 78, 154–55
Pakistan 45, 71, 72, 106, 155
peace
　and security vi, 107, 111
　journalism vi, x, 110
　studies v, 168–70, 172, 174, 176
Peace Boat v, vii, xi, 162, 151–59, 161–62
peacebuilding 157
peacekeeping 114, 119
Pinter, Harold 28

political economy 170

Q

Qabbani, Nizar 10

R

Reconciliation 152, 156, 158
　see also Truth and Reconciliation Commission
reconstruction 36, 104, 106
refugee vii, xx, 33, 37, 47, 68, 79, 85–89, 150, 152
Responsibility to Protect (R2P) 113–20, 185
Rwanda 26, 30, 113–14

S

security
　global 46
　human 34
　international vi, xvi
Shi'a xiv, 66, 69, 70, 78, 99
Sierra Leone x, 115–16, 119
Somali 114
sovereignty xx, 63, 113–14, 117, 128
Stafford, William xvi, 38
Sunni 53, 66, 69–70, 78–79
sustainable/sustainability xi, 151, 154, 162, 165
　development 153
　peace 168, 179
Sydney Peace Foundation vii, ix, 27, 180
Sydney Peace Prize vi, 106

T

Taliban 118
Talisman Sabre 41, 132
terrorism xv, xxi, 28, 38, 67, 72, 97, 106, 107
  war on xv, xx, 72, 106, 118, 158
Truth and Reconciliation Commission xx, 27

U

UNICEF 36, 50
United Nations x, xxii, 41, 92, 93, 99–100, 107, 111, 114, 157, 161, 168

V

violence v–vi, xiii, xv, xvi–xvii, xx, 3, 4, 12, 14, 15, 20–23, 23, 36, 51, 52, 53, 54, 56–58, 62, 127–28, 146, 151, 153, 159, 179
  against women 36–37, 51–63, 122, 128, 159,
  and children 36, 50,
  and foreign policy xiii, 34,
  alternatives to vi, 85–180
  cultural vi
  cultures of xii–xv, 3–15,
  direct 34
  fascination with 3–83
  gendered 36, 51–63, 122
  sacred 14
  structural v, vi
  subjective 58

W

war
  crimes 28, 37, 116–19
  economic costs of 6–8, 38–42
  environmental costs of vi, 33–49
  hidden costs of 39
  human costs of vi, xxii, 33–49, 160
  nuclear costs of 42–45
  post- 35, 104, 116
World Health Organisation (WHO) 36
World War
  I 34
  II 34, 39–40, 91, 98, 103, 151, 155–56

www.ingramcontent.com/pod-product-compliance
Lightning Source LLC
Chambersburg PA
CBHW051124160426
43195CB00014B/2339